D0198940

Presented To:

_____

Presented By:

_____

Date:

_____

words

to live by
for women

Unlock the POWER of Words to
Change Your Life Forever

words

to live by
for women

**Reflections & Insights on the
Most Life-Changing & Thought-
Provoking Words in the Bible**

Words to Live By for Women
ISBN 0-7642-2925-7

Copyright © 2004 by GRQ, Inc.
Brentwood, Tennessee 37027

Published by Bethany House Publishers
11400 Hampshire Avenue South
Bloomington, Minnesota 55438
www.bethanyhouse.com

Bethany House Publishers is a division of Baker Publishing Group, Grand Rapids, Michigan.

Library of Congress Control Number 200401926

Compiler and Editor: Lila Empson
Writer: Janet Bly
Design: Whisner Design Group

04 05 06 / 4 3 2 1

Colors fade, temples
crumble, empires fall, but
wise words endure.

Edward Thorndike

Contents

Introduction

"The right word at the right time is like precious gold set in silver" (Proverbs 25:11 CEV). Words signify ideas and thoughts. Words contain the smallest unit of speech with meaning. The perfect word at a critical time can burst through your priorities and your responsibilities as a woman. Understanding can make sense of your relationships and your need to know yourself. A spiritual vocabulary can help you settle down to both faith-filled peace and forward action.

The Bible is called God's Word because it holds the words of God. God communicates to you through words—a word of faith, a word of chal-

lenge or correction, a word of wisdom or love. Word upon word, you learn who God is and what he wants of you. This volume you hold in your hand is a wordbook, a collection of words from the Bible that relate to your spiritual world, that connect you to God.

When you don't have the energy or clearness of mind to recall everything he has said, you can hold on to one word. When you can't change everything, you can work on one thing, by focusing on a word from him. Meditate on a single word at a time.

I hang on to these words for
dear life! These words hold me
up in bad times.

🔒

Psalm 119:49–50

THE MESSAGE

The Key to Happiness

ac·cept·ance, noun.

1. assent or agreement with a stated position.
2. admiration for an individual's appearance or status.
3. a positive reception.
4. **Biblical:** the favor and approval of an individual by God.
5. **Personal:** the confidence to be yourself because of God's unfailing love.

ac·cept·ance

Well done, good and faithful servant! You have been faithful with a few things; I will put you in charge of many things. Come and share your master's happiness!
Matthew 25:21 NIV

You finally get the job of your dreams. You take notice of what kind of behavior your supervisor expects. You attempt to fulfill all the agreements. You work hard to obey all the rules. But most of all you want to have your boss and your co-workers accept you. Without their acceptance, you feel like a failure. You want more than anything else to feel you belong here, to have your boss like you, to be recognized for your efforts and talents. How can you relax and not be so dependent on the perceived responses by the people around you?

You feel a need for acceptance. You sense it's a key to the freedom to be yourself.

Apodechomai is the Greek word for acceptance, which means "to receive heartily," "to welcome by deliberate and ready reception what is offered." The basis for a whole personality begins with knowing acceptance by God as he created

words *to live by*

you to be. The apostle Paul had a problem with acceptance after becoming a believer because he had persecuted many Christians before. Could he be trusted now? First, he learned to accept himself as he was viewed by God. "By the grace of God I am what I am," he said. Those who look to God alone for approval, for the substance of who they are, can receive each day with confidence and welcome whatever reception comes from others. That acceptance by God rests on what Jesus did on your behalf.

Advertisers take advantage of your desire for acceptance by using flattery in order to get something from you. It's a counterfeit acceptance that's obvious by its excess and its insincerity. Compliments please the part of you that wants to belong and find acceptance by your peers. But seeking God's approval first prevents you from saying and doing things only to find acceptance from others. Using tact and sensitivity, you can express your own preferences and the lifestyle you believe God wants for you and not be intimidated by other people's opinions.

When you know God's love and acceptance, you can accept yourself just as you are, with all your imperfections. You can find the courage to discover who you are inside. Self-knowledge and acceptance helps you feel loved and valued. You know yourself to be a person of worth who has something to offer others. Acceptance by God helps you develop confidence in building

It's one thing to conclude that it's important to live your life without undue concern for what other people think. It's another thing to do it.
JANIS HARRIS

The Key to Happiness

relationships with others, even when you lack verbal, voluntary, out-there-in-plain-view acceptance from them.

Here are suggestions to make sure that you accept your real self. Give thanks often to God for how he created you. Make a daily effort to demonstrate the "God-created" you to your friends and family. Exhibit personal acceptance of the God-created you by learning to be your own best friend, by enjoying your own company, and by being content whether you're alone or in a crowd. Resist peer pressure to do something that doesn't match who you know you are, but graciously receive honest praise and sincere compliments.

> Accept one another, then, just as Christ accepted you, in order to bring praise to God.
> **Romans 15:7** NIV

Acceptance happens when you know that God loves you as you are and you discover the person he created you to be. From that base, you can reach out to others and not be overly concerned with their perceived response to you. It's important to know the real you and live that self in honesty and humility before others, whatever their reaction.

words
to live by

etcetera . . .

Things you might not know about *acceptance:*

❶ Studies indicate that many of the world's leaders who endured pain and humiliation growing up inflicted vengeance upon their people to obtain the "acceptance" they never knew growing up.

❶ Artist Benjamin West first realized his skills while baby-sitting his sister and painting her portrait. When his mother returned, she picked up the drawing and exclaimed, "Why, it's Sally!" Then she kissed her son. His mother's acceptance made him a painter, he said years later.

We will never grow in our relationship with God if we don't have the gumption to become single-minded, bent on pleasing God—and God only.
MICHELE HALSEIDE

We [people-pleasers] may even be tempted to fake our spirituality, which impresses everyone but God.
MICHELE HALSEIDE

Whether we live in the body or move out of it, our goal is to be pleasing to him.
2 Corinthians 5:9
GOD'S WORD

God, thank you for accepting me as your child. Help me to reach out to others with the love you've shown to me and not be concerned about whether the love is returned.
Amen.

a c · c e p t · a n c e

an·ger, noun.

1. a venting of hostility because of injury or insult.
2. a strong emotion of displeasure.
3. active animosity toward a person or thing.
4. *Biblical:* mulling over, cherishing a provocation that should be released to God.
5. *Personal:* excusing or hiding one's own faults by lashing out at others.

an·ger

If someone insults you, God wants you to smile. If anyone stomps on you even seventy times seven, God asks you to forgive. But you're angry because you have been wronged. Why can't you indulge in angry bashing to even the score? It helps to consider the price.

In your anger do not sin: Do not let the sun go down while you are still angry, and do not give the devil a foothold.
Ephesians 4:26–27
NIV

Anger is like a clogged artery in one's relationship with God and people. Anger binges rarely accomplish God's purpose in your life or theirs. Yet anger is a weapon for good or evil.

Anger can defend a righteous cause or mow people down. It can also be a prod. Anger signals something's out of whack that needs to be fixed—inside you or around you. If you didn't have the capacity for anger, you'd be passionless, incapable of righting wrongs. An organization like Mothers Against Drunk Drivers (MADD) is an example of anger translated into positive action.

words
to live by

Channeling a Red-Hot Passion

words

But what is anger? This passion rages with the intent to harm or punish an offending party. Anger seeks restitution. Some anger is sinful, some is not. But all anger needs to be purified by allowing God to search the wounded heart for half-truths, hidden motives, and shared blame. Blindness hampers the angry one's insight.

The Bible warns that most types of human anger smack of selfishness. Here are a couple tests you can give yourself—do you get angry most often about personal slights or over injustices against others? Would your family members call you an angry person? That is, would they say that you can't control your temper, that you tend to argue all the time, and that you lash out at the smallest criticism? The Bible also distinguishes between feelings of anger and acting them out. Anger can range from simple annoyance to vexed to the point of verbal and physical abuse. And the Word of God challenges you that one day is long enough to indulge this emotion.

Think back to the last time you got riled. Did your response match the crime? The most important question you can ask is "Why am I angry?" Anger dims by pleading, "Lord, please change me!" This is your strongest starting point. But be patient with yourself. Give yourself time to work through the trying affront and hand it over to God. Chronic anger doesn't dissipate overnight.

> Our anger can be a tremendous gift, if we dare to look at the feelings it covers up . . . the fears, hurts, resentments, and self-protective motives we work hard to keep out of sight, and to emerge as changed people.
> LARRY CRABB

Channeling a Red-Hot Passion

Meanwhile, work through your ragged feelings by praying for the offenders. Wish God's highest good for them. Try to understand what caused them to say or do this or that. You may not know the whole story and may be prone to misinterpret. Insight is needed for anger to heal, to lose its steam and sting. Find Scriptures that deal with anger and embrace a truth that seeps through the pain. Breathe a silent prayer when your button's been punched. Some find relief when they write a blunt, honest letter to the perpetrator, then tear it up.

If anger runs rampant, it sprays out to people who had nothing to do with the original offense. Combating anger requires not only self-control but forgiveness. And no matter the cause, aim all your energies toward resolving the situation God's way.

❶

You cope with anger when you admit you have a problem, when you define the specific form it takes, then determine the catalyst that set it off. Anger's controlling power over you lessens when you allow yourself to grieve what you lost or endured and release your antagonist to God and his discipline.

You should be quick to listen and slow to speak or to get angry. If you are angry, you cannot do any of the good things that God wants done.
James 1:19–20 CEV

words
to live by

etcetera . . .

Things you might not know about *anger:*

❶ Chronic hostile attitudes can damage the heart muscle, disrupt the heart's rhythm, and cause blood to clot and dislodge plaque that blocks arteries. Fuming silently leads to high blood pressure and depression.

❶ Personality type influences how you handle anger. Type A's are in a hurry, impatient, and often angry. Type B's are laid-back, calm, tend to be good listeners, and are slow to anger.

Sinless anger is never out of control. It does not gratify the sinful desire to nurse personal grievances.
CALVIN MILLER

Beyond being a mark of spiritual maturity, the ability to control your own anger will also allow you to manage your encounters with others who are angry.
CRAIG MASSEY

A gentle answer turns away wrath, but a harsh word stirs up anger.
Proverbs 15:1 NIV

God, help me to understand a situation before I react. Temper my judgments with compassion. Help me as I seek to correct misunderstandings. Calm me down when I'm so easily angered.
Amen.

a n · g e r

less grace mercy love faith goodness
rgiveness peace humble holiness obey repent perfect submit
serve fellowship comforter transformed noble character church

Showers of Manna

bless·ings, noun.

1. anything that gives happiness.
2. prosperity and success.
3. good fortunes.
4. *Biblical:* God's undeserved gifts and favors given out of his love and kindness.
5. *Personal:* unexpected joys or provisions that benefit you or your loved ones.

bless·ings

To wish another person prosperity or success is one of the most unselfish things you can do. If tomorrow morning you could go outside and find any heavenly blessing of your choice poured out of the skies, what would you ask for? Or would you prefer your blessings more localized and controlled rather than streaming down like manna on everyone? "Depends on what the blessings are," you might say.

From the fullness of his grace we have all received one blessing after another. John 1:16 NIV

The Hebrew word *barakah* conveys the idea of a blessing as a gift offered through a powerful utterance. Blessings were oral statements that included deathbed bequests, which had legal authority in ancient Eastern law. In the Greek, *eulogia* means a concrete benefit, a good bestowed either now or in the future, especially from God.

God's blessings never run out; they overlap one another. He keeps generating

words
to live by

new ones. Like any loving parent, it is his delight to pour out blessings upon you. And like any child, sometimes you ignore them or take them for granted. God's blessings are pleasures or advantages for the purpose of bringing goodness into your life. They have another purpose too: to nudge you to the place he wants you to be, in attitude or action. However, their full value may or may not be apparent at the moment you receive them. A conflict arises when you decide what the blessing should be and when and how it should come. The apostle Paul asked three times for his "thorn in the side" to be removed. God told him the thorn was a blessing in disguise, to keep him from becoming conceited.

Your choices can determine the kinds of blessings you receive. Some blessings come as a direct result of obedience to God, and some blessings happen when you share the gospel with someone. Anyone who fears God and tries to please him will enjoy automatic blessings. You are to give out your own blessings whenever you can, especially to those who ill-treat you, out of the store of blessings God gives you. In fact, God's abundant provisions can overwhelm you at times. God's blessings pour from his grace, that love he shows to you that is often so undeserved.

Jesus taught about the blessings of God. His blessings include knowing him, being his child, receiving mercy, becoming righteous, finding comfort, going to heaven. You can impart blessings to the people around you—by providing food, help in times of

Many flowers open to the sun, but only one follows him constantly. Heart, be thou the sunflower, not only open to receive God's blessing, but constant in looking to him.
JEAN PAUL RICHTER

dness grace mercy love faith goodness truth freedom hope
orgiveness peace humble holiness obey repent perfect submit
serve fellowship comforter transformed noble character church

Showers of Manna

As it is written:
"Eye has not seen,
nor ear heard, nor
have entered into
the heart of man
the things which
God has prepared
for those who
love Him."
I Corinthians 2:9
NKJV

trouble, and various kinds of encouragement. And you can bring blessings to God. He delights in those who obey him. He finds pleasure in earnest attempts to seek him and his ways. He enjoys the activities you ask him to join in. He is pleased when you humble yourself.

Right now, list your blessings. Cross out the ones that could be stolen or destroyed, such as anything material, temporal. Circle those that are eternal, that could never be taken from you, such as your salvation, the love you've received or given. Just thinking about God's presence, your friends and family, your permanent blessings, can bring a quiet joy, a feeling of happiness, no matter what else clouds the horizon.

Blessings come from God to everyone on earth—light and rain, breath and love. Special spiritual blessings, such as his daily companionship and the promise of heaven, are poured out only on his children, making them rich with their abundance. It's up to you to notice his blessings, to receive them, and share them whenever you can with the people in your world.

words
to live by

Things you might not know about *blessings:*

❶ Benedictions—or blessings—can be given by a minister or priest to a parishioner, by a parent to a child, or by a friend to another friend. Benedictions are usually words of hope and encouragement that God will impart benefits, favors, protection, and joy on the person being blessed.

❷ A book such as Barbara Ann Kipfer's *14,000 Things to Be Happy About* provides multitudes of lists of daily blessings. It includes such often-taken-for-granted blessings as "seeing the moon rise" and "dozens of places to curl up with a book."

The best things are nearest: breath in your nostrils, light in your eyes, flowers at your feet, duties at your hand, the path of God just before you.
ROBERT LOUIS STEVENSON

It is embarrassing to live in the most comfortable time in history and not be happy. We all have so much!
PEGGY NOONAN

Blessed are all who fear the LORD, who walk in his ways. You will eat the fruit of your labor; blessings and prosperity will be yours.
Psalm 128:1–2 NIV

God, open my eyes to see your blessings to me right now. I want to bask in them, enjoy them to the fullest measure. Show me someone today to whom I can share one of those blessings.
Amen.

b l e s s · i n g s

The Disciplines of Royalty

char·ac·ter, noun.

1. an individual's disposition or reputation.
2. the mettle revealed when tested or tried.
3. integrity or fortitude.
4. **Biblical:** the constant striving for moral and ethical words and actions that imitate Jesus.
5. **Personal:** the complex of traits that define personality.

char·ac·ter

If you've lived long enough, you are known by your character. You can discern how others view your character by the stories that are told about you, the teasing you receive, and also the types of things you are asked to do. Your response to tough situations reveals your character and forms your reputation. However, reputation conjures up only what others perceive you to be from their limited knowledge.

You were born with a character tendency. You also can deter or develop certain character traits. Character includes both natural and acquired attributes or abilities.

You have been created to reflect God's character. He formed you with the ability to be noble, like Ruth. Like the king he is, he wants to discipline you to be his royal daughter. His character includes love that freely blesses, patience that forgives sinners, faithfulness to every

All my fellow towns-
men know that you
are a woman of
noble character.
Ruth 3:11 NIV

words
to live by

promise he makes. The core of his character hinges on the power of his awesome holiness. Your character hangs on willful, learned, though sometimes reluctant, acts of integrity.

Your character is a combined product of your natural personality, your daily habits, and your evolving environment. God's character is different because it is perfect, has never changed, and is untarnished by a single spot of sin. And he can display all his full character in every competing aspect of it at once. He can be just and merciful, holy and loving, all at the same time. You're much more limited. You can be faithful, but cranky. You can tell the truth, but sting with your attitude. That's why you need the two words in your character arsenal: "I'm sorry."

The Bible reveals that persevering through trials and traumas produces character, and character breeds hope. How does that happen? By your willing obedience to follow with vigor how the Lord leads you in a trying circumstance, you build the stamina of trust and confidence in him. A noble character develops by being good, kind, and forgiving with no superior watching you. When all the pretense and pride, along with any need to prove yourself, gets stripped away, you discover who you are.

Being known as a woman of character starts with a change of heart, a desire to be controlled by God's Spirit and the guidance of God's Word to practice the deeds of virtue for a long period of time. Over the

Character is made beautiful by the faithful doing of little things. Everything is of importance, no matter how little it looks, in the building of a soul that is to live with God forever.
CHARLES JEFFERSON

The Disciplines of Royalty

years you reveal your disposition and your moral divides.

There are few earthly accolades for character. No Nobel prizes. No academy awards. No cash bonuses. No Miss Character contests. You can be a material success without it. You can be well liked. You can even be president. But you will never please yourself or God without ethical fiber. People of character serve as society's glue. They keep civility intact. They prevent chaos and anarchy. Relationships are ruled by reason, and rules are reasonably obeyed. A woman of character can unite a family, a church, a community, or, like Joan of Arc, a nation.

The Bereans were of more noble character than the Thessalonians, for they received the message with great eagerness and examined the Scriptures every day to see if what Paul said was true. Acts 17:11 NIV

Character represents your qualities as a person. Your reputation may or may not portray your true character. God wants you to be like him. His goal is to build his character in you. Becoming a woman of character takes years of trials and practice in doing things right. You don't know what character traits you possess until a test of some kind reveals it to you.

words
to live by

Things you might not know about *character:*

❶ Challenging students with solid curriculum plus discipline and self-control, say some, produces a better society of adults. Groups such as the Character Education Partnership, Inc., of Washington, D.C., seek to teach virtues that the majority of people can agree on.

❷ In the nineteenth century, the phrase "hold your horses" was used to encourage the character traits of self-control and patience. It developed out of harness racing. The amateur drivers often started their charges before a race had begun, causing the official to shout, "Hold your horses!"

Character is what a person does when alone, the decisions made away from the persuasions of friends.
PETER MARSHALL

Character is something you are; but it must also be something you desire to become. Ultimately, your character is your mark on society.
STEPHANIE NELSON

Do not be misled: "Bad company corrupts good character."
I Corinthians 15:33 NIV

God, build your character in me. Give me fortitude and courage and integrity in my innermost being.
Amen.

c h a r · a c · t e r

choice, noun.

1. the use of judgment to pick between alternatives.
2. an option that requires an action.
3. a decision or selection that may alter the future.
4. **Biblical:** a test by God that reveals who you are and who you need to become.
5. **Personal:** discernment developed through practice that determines my will from God's will.

c h o i c e

I have offered you life or death, blessings or curses. Choose life so that you and your descendants will live.
Deuteronomy 30:19
GOD'S WORD

You pick up the telephone to make a call. You hear a knock and open the door. You read an ad and send your money or apply for the job. You're invited to an event and you go. You hear of a need and get involved. You get in your car and drive out to the country. Every choice you make sets in motion a set of events that could be a minor blip on your radar screen or change the course of your life.

Choice is the power of preference, the right to select, the liberty to elect. It comes with responsibility to access all the information you can. Many times your choice breeds consequences for other people too. Daily choices should be made with spiritual discernment.

The system of choice is a pattern established by God. He created people with the freedom to choose to either accept his love and his laws or not, to follow his plan and seek his advice or your

words
to live by

A Most Excellent Freedom

own. Choice is necessary to determine whose side you're on. To do good or evil requires a choice. The Bible presents a choice between a narrow gate and a wide road. Only a few find and enter the small opening that leads to eternal life. Choice implies that someone or something is picked out, after careful consideration.

Rebekah made choices that changed her life and many others. When a stranger came to town and asked for a drink, she drew water for his camels too, not knowing the stranger had prayed that the woman who should be Isaac's wife would do that very deed. Then Rebekah chose to leave her family and marry Isaac, whom she'd never met.

The processes of choice produce changes. In learning how to make a choice, you sort out your motives, test your commitments, and mature in discernment. You grow in your knowledge of God as you interact in prayer and study his Word. Perhaps you're confronted with a choice between two alternatives, both of them good. Other times the multiple choice forces you to sort between the better of two evils. When you make a wrong choice, don't despair. Give it to God. Your detour toward destruction did not surprise him. He is the guide to steer you back into his grace-filled purpose.

A choice becomes more difficult if your decision clashes with the status quo. Social pacesetters may try to influence your choice with definite viewpoints of their own. You

> God's will is not loathsome. It is the greatest thing in all of life to get hold of. There is no greater joy or satisfaction than to be in the center of the will of God and know it.
> **PAUL E. LITTLE**

A Most Excellent Freedom

could be ridiculed if you choose an action that departs from accepted behavior, such as refusing to date an unbeliever or deciding not to touch alcohol. Sometimes you fight against your own natural desires. Standards can be swayed by whom you're trying to please.

To make a right moral choice requires being transformed in your thinking. Other times it means action, such as returning to a situation from which you've been running. When you make a God-honoring decision that brings about decided differences in your life or others, it's a sign of spiritual maturity.

> You did not choose me, but I chose you and appointed you to go and bear fruit—fruit that will last.
>
> John 15:16 NIV

God gave you the power of choice, to test whether you'd go his way or your own. The choices you make affect more than yourself. The spiritual process of making choices develops discernment and draws you closer to God.

words
to live by

Things you might not know about *choice:*

❶ Psychologists note that those who hop from job to job or relationship to relationship need to figure out that the problem is not to make a better choice, but to change themselves. Self-examination is crucial.

❶ With the explosion of choice in products, services, and lifestyles, moderns are pushed to want the best of everything. A choice that used to take five minutes now takes days.

God is always pushing us, saying, "Take the next step—go down this new path."
MADELEINE L'ENGLE

Scripture seems to emphasize staying close to our Guide. Close to him, we are on the right track, even if we cannot see where we are going.
ALISON A. McCAUGHAN

Ask and you'll get;
Seek and you'll find;
Knock and the door will open.
Luke 11:9 THE MESSAGE

God, help me pull free from the glitzy words that lead to dried-up dreams and dead ends. Purify my wrongheaded notions as I seek your counsel. Change me.
Amen.

choice

A Voluntary Act

com·mit·ment, noun.

1. a pledge to do something.
2. an obligation, a duty.
3. an engagement by contract.
4. **Biblical:** a vow made before God.
5. **Personal:** a promise made that cannot be broken without repercussions.

com·mit·ment

You are known and shaped by your commitments, and your first and foremost commitment is to God. Keeping your commitments brings honor to him.

Commitment is remembering the promises you made and making only the promises you can keep. The Hebrew word *neder* indicates a verbal consecration. This word is used in service of God, such as vowing to perform, to make an offering, or to abstain from something. *Commitment* is a binding of yourself to God in a matter by making a public statement in order to be held accountable. To make a commitment is not a religious duty, but a voluntary act. However, once made it should be kept for your integrity's sake and the expectations and needs of others. Ruth chose commitment to her mother-in-law, Naomi, even though her husband was dead: "Your people will be my people and your God my God," she said. On the strength of that commitment,

It is dangerous to make a rash promise to God before counting the cost.
Proverbs 20:25 NLT

words
to live by

Ruth earned the respect of Naomi's people and the attentions of Boaz, and she comforted a bitter old woman.

The Bible word *covenant* decrees a commitment, that is, it establishes a relationship, and is usually initiated by God. The power to keep a covenant comes from God, by his writing his laws on your heart, or by your allowing his Spirit to work in you.

Commitment is more than a fuzzy feeling that merely celebrates a moment with "maybe" or "let's try this out to see if it works." True commitment happens when you understand the rewards for making it happen and the consequences when it breaks down. The committed persevere through inconvenience, hard times, and obstacles to get to the other side. Sickness means you come alongside to nurse or help find treatment. Financial setbacks draw forth your creative thriftiness. Misunderstanding forces you to talk it all out.

True commitment says "I will" and backs it up by being there when you said you would. Commitment signals that the partnership is vital to some bigger purpose. Commitment forges a sane and secure path through the thorny thicket of relationships. You're nudged to concentrate your energies on follow-through, forgiveness, and getting it right. Commitment encourages you to take time to address the concerns of family, church, or community when it's uniquely your role. You learn to listen as well as speak your own heart because of a firm promise.

When you make a commitment, you hold nothing back. You give everything

It is very important that we made vows before God that we would stay together—in sickness and health, for richer or poorer; for good things, bad things.
MADELEINE L'ENGLE

A Voluntary Act

you've got to your God-appointed cause and the persons he has led you to. This creates a small sanctuary of trust that contrasts with and challenges the larger complex of loose connections. You hang on, with God's help, through the unpredictability of tests and trials.

Someone somewhere depends on you. Your commitment empowers your co-worker, steadies your friend. Knowing you'll keep your word may save a family member from grief or confusion. Commitment makes sure you seek God for the courage and wisdom you need to forge ahead with whatever it takes.

> Once the commitment is clear, you do what you can, not what you can't. The heart regulates the hands.
>
> **2 Corinthians 8:12**
> THE MESSAGE

Commitment to people grows out of your commitment to God, to build faithful relationships and complete important tasks. Commitment is a promise to be there for the people who need you, so they can trust you when times get tough. It is a God-inspired preference for this one or that group over others when lines must be drawn. They know whose side you're on. They can rest with complete trust in your word.

words
to live by

etcetera . . .

Things you might not know about *commitment:*

❶ In studies of couples happily married for thirty years or longer, the keys seem to be their commitment to stay together, plus development of communication skills for conflict management. Candor and respect result when each partner knows they're in it for the long run.

❶ Commitment affects attitudes that color the approach to jobs and relationships, causing a positive take on the quirks of co-workers and the faults of friends and mates.

Whenever you and I make and keep a promise we are as close to being like God as we can ever be.
LEWIS B. SMEDES

Without being bound to the fulfillment of our promises, we would never be able to keep our identities.
HANNAH ARENDT

Ruth replied, "Don't urge me to leave you or to turn back from you. Where you go I will go, and where you stay I will stay."
Ruth 1:16–17 NIV

God, it is so hard to stay committed when I have been hurt deeply or when I'm weary from trying. Please give me some encouragement to attempt another act of love, one more kindness. Amen.

c o m · m i t · m e n t

The Polite Kind of Love

com·pro·mise, noun.

1. a settlement of conciliation.
2. the result of mutual concessions.
3. a happy medium between conflicting courses.
4. **Biblical:** foregoing nonessentials for the unity of the body of Christ.
5. **Personal:** readjustment of your position for more positive, godly results.

com · pro · mise

To those who are weak, I became weak so I could win the weak. I have become all things to all people so I could save some of them in any way possible.

1 Corinthians 9:22 NCV

There's some flexibility for the Christian, a place and a purpose for compromise. If you don't sacrifice central biblical truth or basic spiritual principle, but want to reach out to somebody of a different culture or custom, there're ways to develop various accents of love. You can be at home with people who are at odds with you if you determine what's important and stick to it. On the other hand, you can decipher what's peripheral and surrender your best arguments in quiet debate or silence. The healthiest compromise centers on a giving up of your tastes, your convenience, some innocent pleasure, an interest, even a right, in order to accomplish a valuable spiritual purpose in another's life.

Unity and peace among the family of God is exhorted in the Bible. At certain junctures of conflict, compromise can produce sweet harmony. *Compromise* is

words
to live by

agreement through giving something up. Compromise is necessary between Christians in order to settle nondoctrinal disputes with a peaceable spirit. Spiritual purposes should always be in the forefront of handling confrontations on nonessentials, rather than proving you are right. Discernment is needed to know when to back away or when to forego an advantage or pleasure for the sake of peace. On the other hand, there are times to make a stand, even when you have to confront someone, as the apostle Paul did to Peter. Paul confronted Peter for his lack of courage and hypocrisy. The stakes involved should determine your course of action.

Unfortunately, compromise can be used for mere convenience, shady deals, or immediate profits. You can strain to please everyone about everything for monetary gain. You placate others in order to forestall change or to prevent disturbing controversy for one's own momentary peace of mind. Compromise in the world is more like appeasement, when you buy somebody's vote or pacify them with lucrative concessions. Compromise can then come at the expense of principles or morals. Expediency is the highest virtue.

The Christian woman remains who she is in a foreign castle as well as in her own condo, sticking by her biblical standards, yet showing respect to those who are unlike her. She defines herself by her moral beliefs. For her, compromise is flexibility on nonessential matters. It is love as sterling politeness, ready to defer with dignity to

> Compromise, if not the spice of life, is its solidity. It is what makes nations great and marriages happy.
> PHYLLIS McGINLEY

con·tent·ment, noun.

1. ease of mind.
2. pleased with things as they are.
3. a comfortable geniality.
4. *Biblical:* the knowledge of the presence and grace of the Lord.
5. *Personal:* complete acceptance of what God is doing and providing for you.

con·tent·ment

I have learned the secret of being content in any and every situation, whether well fed or hungry, whether living in plenty or in want.
Philippians 4:12 NIV

If you're like the average American, you own twice as much stuff as your parents did. You probably earn more money than your mother could. You may have solved the challenge of how to make a career. You're surrounded by luxuries. You eat out three times more often, own more cars, and travel more. You possess more rights and freedoms as a woman. But do you experience contentment, that is, the sense that "I have everything I need"? Or are you constantly looking to the future, thinking, "If I can just do this or have that, I'll be happy"?

The apostle Paul learned contentment through all kinds of circumstances. The Hebrew word for contentment is *sabea,* which means "to have one's fill of," "to have desires satisfied," even "to have in excess." *Contentment* is to be comfortable with your means, your lot in life. The poor can have it; the rich might not.

words
to live by

Contentment purports pleasure in who you are, what you have, and where God has placed you. The Word of God emphasizes that if you have the basics in life, food and clothing, that's all you need to be content. Contentment centers on your relationship with God, how close you are to him, how well you know him.

All kinds of pressures keep you from being content—because you don't possess this thing or you don't look like that person or you lack a certain ability. Refusing to dwell on comparisons, developing a generous spirit toward the attributes of others, provides greed controls. Otherwise, you'll only tolerate what you have until you get more.

If you lack contentment, it may be because you don't recognize all the "extras" that you've been given. Go spend a week camped out in a tent or take a walk in the poorer side of town, and then come back and look at what you own by this new perspective. Contentment is not common because it must be learned. Contentment grows out of fellowship with God. He wants to fill you with satisfaction. But that might come only after a season of suffering of the soul that purifies your passions and priorities.

Contentment is a biblical command. That doesn't mean you can't pursue ambitions and dreams, but you'll enjoy the journey and the completion better if you grasp contentment along the way. If you have no contentment with what you have now,

> Christian contentment is that sweet, inward, quiet, gracious frame of spirit, which freely submits to and delights in God's wise and fatherly disposal in every condition.
> J. BURROUGHS

ness grace mercy love faith goodness truth freedom hope
orgiveness peace humble holiness obey repent perfect submit
serve fellowship comforter transformed noble character church

A Learned Art

We didn't bring anything into this world, and we won't take anything with us when we leave. So we should be satisfied just to have food and clothes.
I Timothy 6:7–8
CEV

you're not likely to find it when you receive what you desire.

You know you're contented if you're settled down inside, if you're able to either stay or go and not experience emotional turmoil. The sign of contentment is a quiet, still heart. You find contentment by slowing down and accepting the doing of each duty one at a time, in its season. The contented find joy in simple things. The state of your contentment provides a crucial test of what's important to you. You still persevere in prayer and fight for what's right, but you'll be satisfied that God has given you everything you need for your present happiness.

🔒

Contentment is the ability to enjoy your life as it is. However, it may take some rough experiences to learn that state, to jostle you into seeing your life with new eyes. Getting close to God purifies the desires for masses of worldly goods and gain, so you can appreciate little things.

words
to live by

Things you might not know about *contentment:*

❶ The late Ng Eng Teng, considered one of Singapore's foremost sculptors, portrayed the rare wedded theme of "Wealth and Contentment" in one of his inspirational biomorphic forms. Ng's sculptures embody basic feelings and states of mind in a search for meaning in a materialistic world.

❷ Counselor Paul Welter encourages nursing home workers who deal with those suffering memory loss or disorientation to emphasize "the meaning of the moment." Contentment comes for nurse and patient when they attach significance to present acts of love given and received.

Whatever my lot, thou hast taught me to say, "It is well, it is well with my soul."
HORATIO G. SPAFFORD

Be content with such things as ye have.
Hebrews 13:5 KJV

Contentment: agreeing with God that he and what he has provided for you are sufficient for his purposes for you.
GAYLE ROPER

God, still my inordinate passions for temporal things. As I rest before you in this moment, fill me with your Spirit. I rest contented in your presence, your will, your provisions.
Amen.

con·tent·ment

Cheer for the Job Ahead

cour·age, noun.

1. the determination to do right when pressured to do wrong.
2. the facing of danger with eyes wide open.
3. reserves of moral strength in times of crisis.
4. *Biblical:* obeying God despite the risks or losses.
5. *Personal:* ability to perform acts of bravery while overcoming fear and feelings of inadequacy

c o u r · a g e

In 1950 Florence Chadwick became the first woman to swim across the English Channel in a record thirteen hours, twenty-three minutes. A year later she tried it again, but this time fog and adverse winds railed against her. She couldn't see the land. She felt heavy discouragement as she strained her muscles to keep going. She had to take medicine for seasickness. Finally, her attitude changed and she regained her mental and physical strength as she focused her mind on the vision of the shoreline. She mustered up courage for the last miles by forging all her thoughts on the end goal.

Be strong and of good courage, do not fear nor be afraid of them; for the LORD your God, He is the One who goes with you.
Deuteronomy 31:6
NKJV

Courage is a quality of mind or spirit that enables you to face danger with self-possession, confidence, and resolution. Spiritual courage displays itself in vigor of moral character in times of emergency. A woman of courage is energetic as she executes administrative power for the task at hand, while few may know her inner

words
to live by

struggles. She speaks freely, with authority, in frank, open terms. She takes a public stand for what's right, no matter the consequences. She boldly faces the next step. She can do acts of courage even though fears and doubts may assail her.

Although most people admire courage, they may also dote on keeping you in your place. "It can't be done," "you've messed up before," and "who do you think you are" are the frequent mantras intoned. Courage enables Christian discipleship in a world of temptations, peer pressures, and dangers. There are times when you stand out from the crowd because you won't do something that everyone else seems to do, with no feelings of constraint.

The Hebrew word *ruach*, for *courage*, is the same as the word for *spirit*. *Courage* is the spunk to conquer your own despair or fears in order to accomplish good over evil. You can stir up courage through prayer, reading God's Word, and watching other brave souls. The primary source of courage is the power of the Holy Spirit in you. With him, you can face down any obstacle. Courage comes in the process of obedience to God. Acting on courage helps you conquer your inner demons.

When God requires courage from you, he has a spiritual purpose to be fulfilled that may or may not be evident at that moment. As you forge ahead, he fights your enemies for you. Courage gets you into the act while you leave the results to God. The highest

> Above all, we must realize that no arsenal, or no weapon in the arsenals of the world, is so formidable as the will and moral courage of free men and women.
> **RONALD REAGAN**

Cheer for the Job Ahead

acts of spiritual courage are meant to draw the world's attention to Jesus.

To find courage, you need to discover a bit of hope in a desperate situation. Courage comes from full confidence in God's goodness and in God as the sovereign Lord over all the details of your life. But sometimes the most courage is needed to simply wait on him and his timing, especially when the fog of despair rolls in and you lose sight of your mission. Meanwhile, you can offer the blessing of courage to someone else by your intercessions and role model. Courage pumps the heart and spirit with cheer for the job when the winds of adversity blow.

Courage is moral and spiritual stamina. It takes courage to live the Christian life in a world bent on knocking you down and expecting you to fail. Courage comes from trust that God will deliver you one way or another, in his timing. Courage grows beyond mental belief to produce action that helps conquer the quaking doubts you may feel.

When the disciples saw him walking on the lake, they were terrified. "It's a ghost," they said, and cried out in fear. But Jesus immediately said to them: "Take courage! It is I. Don't be afraid."
Matthew 14:26–27
NIV

words
to live by

Things you might not know about *courage:*

❶ Saint Theresa of Avila vowed to live for God alone. In response, the Inquisition ordered that both she and her writings be seized "for examination." Despite illness and death threats, she submitted herself to their intense pressure and scrutiny and still spearheaded a vast spiritual revival.

❶ Amy Carmichael worked in India to save young girls from cult prostitution. She faced material need, pain, disease, disappointments, and even attacks by friends. But she wrote of the courage she found in God's presence.

The Christian who sings in the night proves to be a courageous character. It is the bold Christian who can sing God's sonnets in the darkness.
CHARLES HADDON SPURGEON

God's path to victory for you and me is to decide *now* to be strong and courageous.
KAY ARTHUR

Keep alert. Be firm in your faith. Stay brave and strong. Show love in everything you do.
1 Corinthians 16:13–14 CEV

God, sometimes I'm reluctant to speak out or take action on behalf of certain causes or people who need an advocate. Guide me in the works I need to do and the words I should say.
Amen.

cour·age

49

Becoming a Work of Art

des·ti·ny, noun.

1. a course of events beyond the power or control of humans.
2. the goal at the end of life's road.
3. the object toward which one strives.
4. *Biblical:* the reason why God created you.
5. *Personal:* God's will for your life accomplished when you give him full access.

d e s·t i·n y

You have that sense of life passing you by. You hear that voice, the one that whispers, "You're not doing what you were born to do." Is this the voice of God nudging you to complete your destiny?

The Bible relates accounts of individuals and nations fulfilling their God-given destiny. Your destiny is the purpose for which you were created, the end for which you are headed, the reason why you exist. *Destiny* is that succession or series of events that leads to a God-honoring conclusion. You can reject and try to thwart God's destiny for you because God gives you free will. You've got choices all along the road. However, his destiny for all believers in Christ swells with nothing but good intentions. He will give you chances to redirect your detours and keep you headed toward that perfect purpose, in spite of the rebellions of your heart.

Without a personal, loving God behind it all, destiny seems like a random,

I have raised you up for this very purpose, that I might show you my power and that my name might be proclaimed in all the earth.
Exodus 9:16 NIV

words
to live by

irreversible, impersonal force that predetermines where you live, who you meet, and what you accomplish. It's your lot in life, and there's nothing you can do about it. It's kismet, or fate. It's your fortune or your doom. In contrast, the Christian's destiny unfolds under the care and vision of a loving God who longs for your cooperation. It's a tandem working out between a daughter and her heavenly Father.

God is your final destiny. Meanwhile, destiny is anything God leads you to do, from giving a cool drink in his name, to traveling across the world to evangelize a village. It is stretching to your God-given potential by contributing to the welfare of someone in need.

Jesus fulfilled his ultimate human destiny on the cross. He also completed his divine purpose by the many deeds he accomplished. "I have glorified You on the earth," he told the Father. "I have finished the work which You have given Me to do" (John 17:4 NKJV).

You find your destiny by inviting God into your everyday details, through listening for his voice and staying alert to his interventions. Ideas and dreams that refuse to go away, no matter how many months or years pass, may be signs of a divine purpose. In addition, perhaps you're steered to a special place. Or faced with a perplexing problem. Or appointed to a privileged position. Or blessed with a pointed prayer or prophetic word. Or impelled by a project. Or paired

> We should ask ourselves when the problems of providence distress us: what is God's ultimate end in His dealings with His children? . . . It is the *glory of God Himself*.
> J. I. PACKER

ness grace mercy love faith goodness truth freedom hope
orgiveness peace humble holiness obey repent perfect submit
serve fellowship comforter transformed noble character church

Becoming a Work of Art

with a potent partner. Or you're burdened to reach out to a particular person or people.

Fulfilling your destiny is not for your mere enjoyment, though it will bring you much satisfaction. It makes you part of some aspect of God's greater plan. Your destiny molds your life into a work of art, a beautiful showcase for his glory, in spite of your faults.

God's destiny for you applies for all eternity, as well as works out through circumstances here on earth. God's destiny for you plays out as you yield your will to his. Destiny is God calling your name, saying, "Come be with me. I have something to tell you."

All the stages of my life were spread out before you, the days of my life all prepared before I'd even lived one day.
Psalm 139:16
THE MESSAGE

You've got the freedom to make decisions, and God has a plan for your life. Destiny is a specific task created for you by the master designer. Your destiny opens through the abilities God gives you, by the desire he stirs in you to do certain things, through the people he brings alongside you, and by the situations that surround you.

words
to live by

Things you might not know about *destiny:*

❶ Corrie ten Boom found her destiny in a concentration camp during World War II. Before her sister, Betsie, died there, she told Corrie: "Don't forget—a home for the broken ones and our message about God's love that we discovered in this brutal darkness."

❶ In the evenings, when their nine children were in bed, Leo Tolstoy's wife would painstakingly copy out her husband's handwriting of his novels. "The feeling that I can be useful to a great man multiplies my strength tenfold," she would say.

We are in the hands of a loving, un-defeatable omnipotence, and if daily we try to do God's will as we perceive it we shall find mental peace.
LESLIE WEATHERHEAD

We are God's workmanship, created in Christ Jesus to do good works, which God prepared in advance for us to do.
Ephesians 2:10 NIV

A picture is being painted, for me. . . . If I saw the pattern in advance, a sort of schema for "paint-by-numbers," that would leave no room for faith.
PHILLIP YANCEY

God, lead me toward your purpose with the people who cross my path, the conversations I have, and the deeds you nudge me to do. Work in me, through me, and in spite of me.
Amen.

d · e · s · t · i · n · y

The Gift That Refreshes

words

en·cour·age·ment, noun.

1. an incitement to action.
2. the giving of comfort in time of loss.
3. the urging forward by persuasion.
4. **Biblical:** the coming alongside a faltering believer to empower for service.
5. **Personal:** spiritually uplifting others by words or deeds that renew their resolve to keep trying.

en·cour·age·ment

May our Lord Jesus Christ Himself, and our God and Father . . . comfort your hearts and establish you in every good word and work.
2 Thessalonians 2:16–17 NKJV

words
to live by

She's got deadlines and back orders. She's distressed over finances and health issues. She's anxious and fearful about a potential crisis. One more bit of bad news and she feels she'll crumple. Then, the Lord allows you to be her angel of mercy, to relieve her burden. You offer a word of praise. She cries with relief. You have just entered the ministry of encouragement.

Encouragement sets a spirit free to handle harassments and to face life's foes.

The Greek word for *encouragement* is *parakaleo*, which is similar to *paraclete*, which signifies the ministry of God's Spirit to come alongside the believer as an advocate or comforter. *Encouragement* is coming alongside someone else to lift her up, to give her enough hope to keep going.

When the angel Gabriel told Mary the startling news that she, an unmarried woman, would become pregnant with

Jesus, he also advised her to go visit her relative Elizabeth. The angel knew that Elizabeth was pregnant under unusual circumstances too, after being barren into her old age. Elizabeth could empathize with Mary's social embarrassment, could advise her in practical matters, could be a friend. Elizabeth gave just the right encouragement at a very stressful time in Mary's life.

Encouragement is emotional or physical support. Encouragement is rewarding someone for her efforts. It is reaching out to a person who feels downcast or awkward. It is asking questions that show you notice and care.

Real encouragement says, "You have options" or "You're not alone" or "I think your idea's a good one—go for it!"

You know what a gift it is to receive encouragement, but it takes effort to remember to offer it. When someone's name comes to your mind and she did something for you or others that was appreciated, let her know right then with a call or note. You can provide encouragement by praise for a person's abilities or about how she handled a certain situation. If someone's hurting, tell her, "I'm praying for you today." Encouragement pays more attention to a person's strengths than her weaknesses. Encouragement comes with pats on the back or hugs at the end of a long day. It takes courage, the middle word of encouragement, the boldness to enter into another's hardships with a positive action. Your brave words can impart

During a time of heartache and crisis, words can be a life preserver to someone in murky waters. Comforting expressions of kindness and concern will be treasured and mentally replayed again and again.
DEBBIE BARR

The Gift That Refreshes

courage to keep going for the recipient.

Your faith encourages others with hope at the same time that they try to encourage you. Even your attitude in the midst of unpleasant circumstances brings encouragement to others to be more fearless to live their own lives. Those who visit patients in the hospital sometimes come away having been cheered up themselves.

May the God who gives endurance and encouragement give you a spirit of unity among yourselves as you follow Christ Jesus.
Romans 15:5 NIV

The cause of Christ is greatly benefited by encouragers. You receive encouragement through give-and-take in the fellowship of believers, by involvement in a local church. You learn encouragement when you ask God's Spirit to show you how to come alongside with a word or deed that refreshes and renews.

❶

Encouragement gets timid people going with their talents and tasks. Encouragers also develop courage as they get close to another people to boost their spirits. Many are in need of encouragement, so they won't give up. Your encouragement will strengthen the weak when you emphasize their strong points. Work to find right words and loving actions for those who lack confidence or are downcast around you today.

words
to live by

Things you might not know about *encouragement:*

❶ The Foundation for Community Encouragement is a non-profit organization founded to teach the principles of community building to individuals and organizations. Community building principles teach people to come together in ways that provide wholeness in relationships.

❶ Richard D. Lavoie, an authority on learning disabilities, has spent more than thirty years teaching kids to learn, and has discovered that encouragement works best for motivation when it's sincere, when it's focused on a specific effort, and shows personal interest in the individual.

Now more than ever may be the time when you can be the one who helps another person face her present and future with boldness and confidence.
CATHARINE E. ROLLINS

There is nothing better than the encouragement of a good friend.
KATHARINE BUTLER HATHAWAY

Make me [Paul] truly happy by agreeing wholeheartedly with each other, loving one another, and working together with one heart and purpose.
Philippians 2:2 NLT

God, I have received so much encouragement.
Nudge me to do the same for those around me. Fill
my heart and mouth with hope that spills out to
weary ones who might not feel appreciated.
Amen.

en·cour·age·ment

The Certain Opponent

en·e·mies, noun.

1. destructive influences.
2. persons who wish you injury.
3. rivals in love or ambition.
4. **Biblical:** anyone opposing God and his plan.
5. **Personal:** a hostile force or foe that opposes your best interests.

en·e·mies

If you are a follower of Jesus Christ, while you are guaranteed many blessings, you also receive one curse (that can also be converted to a blessing): you will have enemies.

Love your enemies and pray for anyone who mistreats you. Then you will be acting like your Father in heaven.
Matthew 5:44–45 CEV

You have one constant, vigilant enemy who "prowls around like a roaring lion looking for someone to devour," for no other reason than you belong to Jesus. In the Bible, enemies are those on the side of Satan against God. Enemies are anyone who attempts to obstruct God's will, or destroy God's people, of whom Satan is the prime suspect. Enemies include those who persecute you in some way because of your faith. Enemies can be as up close and personal as members of your own household.

Queen Esther had an enemy. Haman, a high official in her husband's court, didn't hate her personally, but he wanted to destroy her people, so she was forced to oppose him. It took all her courage,

words *to live by*

inventiveness, and spiritual resources to overcome Haman and his plots.

You know your enemies by their deceitful words and actions. Enemies betray. Enemies stab you in the back. But enemies don't always stay that way. They can become friends or allies. And enemies can teach you some painful truths about yourself as they often hit you on your blind side. Listen to what your enemies tell you, and pay attention to a kernel of truth that can help you improve a fault. In that way, they can bless you. Look for a positive opening to build a bridge of peace, understanding, or some kind of truce. And ask God to produce a spiritual purpose, no matter what they do. God is good at turning evil on its head by thwarting the intent, as he proved so well by the cross of Christ.

Sometimes a thin line might exist in your mind between who's a real enemy and who's just contrary or mean. You may consider your enemies anyone you don't happen to like. Enemies are people who wish you harm when opposing you. In any case, Jesus' approach to enemies is the same, and it contradicts human nature. It seems as though you should avenge yourself against them, pay them back, at least have nothing to do with them. Jesus exhorts you to love them, pray for them, and meet their specific needs when you can—a cup of cold water, perhaps, or a plate of hot food. Any kindness is encouraged in response to insults. And you're not to gloat when your enemy falls.

The satisfaction and security of any other person, including that of my enemy, must become as significant to me as my own satisfaction and security.
RICHARD WURMBRAND

59

The Certain Opponent

Knowing what to do about enemies becomes more complicated if they invade your country or violently attack you. You can ask God's wisdom and specific direction. Dealing with enemies will never be easy, but rewards come if you do everything you can to treat them in the biblical way. Only God can empower you to do that.

God may send you blessings right in front of your enemies, where they can witness his goodness to you and perhaps turn to him because of it. When you make peace with your enemies, it's a sign of the Lord's work in your life.

O

Everyone has enemies, especially if you're a believer in Jesus Christ. God's Word teaches you how to treat your foes, how to respond to hostility. Ask God to empower you to love those who spite you. Be alert to the fact that enemies can become friends and friends can become enemies.

If someone takes unfair advantage of you, use the occasion to practice the servant life. No more tit-for-tat stuff. Live generously.

Luke 6:30
THE MESSAGE

words
to live by

Things you might not know about *enemies*:

❶ King David seemed to possess a myriad of enemies. He constantly prayed to God about them. The words *enemy* and *enemies* are recorded ninety-three times in the book of Psalms. The words *friend* or *friends* account for only ten mentions.

❶ After the carnage of the Civil War, and after the deaths of Jefferson Davis, president of the Confederacy, and Ulysses Grant, a general on the Union side, their widows settled down near each other. Varina Davis and Julia Grant became the closest of friends.

In no way can a vicious enemy hurt you as much as you hurt yourself by not loving that enemy.
SAINT AUGUSTINE OF HIPPO

If God be for us, it matters not who may be against us.
HANNAH WHITALL SMITH

When we please the Lord, even our enemies make friends with us.
Proverbs 16:7 CEV

God, help me treat my enemies with your love.
As I reach out, free me from the attitudes that
seek to harm them back. May you fight my
true enemies your way, in your time.
Amen.

en · e · mies

A Question of Overcoming

e·vil, noun.

1. a malicious injury.
2. a choice that's morally unacceptable.
3. a diabolic scheme.
4. **Biblical:** rebellion against God's love, holiness, and revealed will.
5. **Personal:** any action that causes spiritual harm or destruction.

e · vil

We do not wrestle against flesh and blood, but against principalities, against powers, against the rulers of the darkness of this age, against spiritual hosts of wickedness in the heavenly places.
Ephesians 6:12 NKJV

She was born rich and in charge as a proud Phoenician princess. She was powerful enough to have prophets killed. She was smart enough to devise clever schemes. She was arrogant enough to oppose God. She's known by scholars as the wickedest woman in the world, the Lady Macbeth of the Bible. She's Jezebel. Her very name symbolizes evil.

The most persistent questions focus on why God allows evil. Two facts remain after all the possible reasons are discussed: God is good, all-wise, and all-powerful, plus he gives humans the option to choose between good and evil. This somehow accomplishes his cosmic spiritual purpose.

The various derivative Hebrew words for *evil* mean "to break to pieces, smash, crush." Evil intends to hurt so bad it destroys. Evil begins with pride, envy, and selfish ambition. Evil is any activity that seeks to ruin life, virtue, or God's purposes.

words
to live by

The word *evil* is difficult to define or even discuss in modern society. It's a primitive term, like talking about the devil and his red suit and pitchfork. That's a convenient cop-out when enjoying easy, comfortable times. But evil in action disrupts this assessment. The word *evil* comes into vogue again when there's no other way to make sense of a horrific event.

Overcome evil with good, the Bible says. One of your spiritual challenges is to discern the difference between good and evil. You can be trained through a study of God's Word. You can practice by sorting out the masses of material thrown at you by the media. The trick is to know enough to recognize evil, yet be innocent of all the seductive influences that attempt to persuade you it's no big deal and actually fun and that introduce inventive ways of doing it.

The problem with evil is, if you study its source and follow the dots, you discover its tentacles everywhere, including your own heart. If God should rid the earth of evil, no one would survive. The ultimate war between good and evil battles inside the human heart. Evil demands a war of wills and spiritual weapons, whether it's coming against you or your loved ones, or it's inside of you. Ask God's Spirit to indwell you. Overcome evil with personal holiness.

Children are born knowing perfectly well that evil exists. Not even the most gently reared child escapes nightmares of the Thing Under the Bed.
SUSAN WISE BAUER

A Question of Overcoming

The encroachment of evil is best stopped early. The practice of evil becomes a habit that's difficult to break. No one suddenly stumbles into evil addictions. It's a progression of choices, a sequence of giving in. You fight evil in the little choices, the hidden thoughts. Evil evolves through steps, through concessions that lead to a logical end out of the mind of the perpetrator, but bring shock to those who see only the final result. You fight evil with the weapons of the light of truth, with righteous living, with the gospel message, with your fertile faith, with the gift of salvation, with the expounding of God's Word, and with all kinds of prayer. You overcome evil with discipline, perhaps slowly, by inches. You defeat evil when you surrender your will and being to the power of Jesus.

Hate what is wrong. Stand on the side of the good. . . . Don't let evil get the best of you, but conquer evil by doing good.
Romans 12:9, 21
NLT

🔒

The presence of evil in the world is a great concern for any compassionate woman. Evil threatens you, your loved ones, and your community. But evil not only exists "out there," it also exists inside your own heart. If you don't overcome evil, it will overwhelm you. Only God and his presence of goodness in your life will neutralize its effects.

words
to live by

Things you might not know about *evil*:

❶ In the early days of the Christian church, conversion and baptism included exorcism of demons and a clear renunciation of Satan, as well as giving of oneself to the Lord. Evangelism was seen as a battle between the forces of light and darkness, good and evil.

❶ Jerry Johnston, author of *The Edge of Evil*, says that 10 percent of American youth are involved with some form of the occult, such as fantasy games, séances, horror films, or horoscopes.

God judged it better to bring good out of evil than to suffer no evil to exist.
SAINT AUGUSTINE OF HIPPO

If you cannot hate evil, you cannot love good.
STRUTHERS BURT

The one who is in you is greater than the one who is in the world.
1 John 4:4 NIV

God, deliver me and my loved ones from evil. Show me what I can do today to restrain evil's influence in my life. Flood me with your goodness.
Amen.

e · v i l

faith, noun.

1. confidence in the truth or value of a person, idea, or thing.
2. trust in God.
3. an opinion, a creed, a doctrine.
4. *Biblical:* a hearty reliance upon God and his promise of salvation through Christ.
5. *Personal:* confidence that God is at work on your behalf.

faith

Mary had faith. When the angel reported the astounding news that she, a virgin, would bear a son, she assented: "Let it be to me according to your word." Mary believed God knew what was best even when what he asked didn't make sense to her human way of thinking. The Roman centurion had faith too. He believed Jesus could heal his servant by just giving the order, by saying the words, because he understood the power of authority.

Rahab the harlot also had faith. She welcomed spies into her home and helped them because she had witnessed and acknowledged the proof that God was on their side. Both saints and sinners can exhibit faith.

The Greek word for *faith, pistis,* signifies "firm persuasion," "trust," "fidelity to," "assurance of." Faith is required in a trusting relationship with an invisible God. Faith means you're persuaded of the

By entering through faith into what God has always wanted to do for us—set us right with him, make us fit for him—we have it all together with God.
Romans 5:1
THE MESSAGE

Bright Hope for Tomorrow

words
to live by

existence of an out-of-sight spiritual world. Strong faith is a weapon in spiritual warfare. It will "be able to quench all the fiery darts of the wicked." Faith grows to a firm conviction by steady experience, by proving God's promises. It helps you persevere in the really tough situations, when you think you'll never make it until tomorrow.

When your faith is observed by others through some outward expression—such as a word you say in conversations or your presence at church—a neighbor or coworker may give more attention to your denominational preference or to a set of doctrines, formulas, or systems of rituals you ascribe to. They'll want to peg you with a group or align you with a leader. But true faith cuts through all these externals to a personal relationship with God. Faith is trusting God's being with all the perplexities of life, no matter how devastating or depressing they might be.

Everyone has faith in something or you couldn't navigate through a day. You believe that most cars will stop for pedestrians. You trust the ground won't drop. You're persuaded a meteor won't hit you. Faith always has an object. You have faith in drivers, firm ground, or percentages. It's the dependability of who or what you have faith in that determines the outcome. Spiritual faith replies, "Whatever happens, I know God loves me and will be with me. I trust him."

> Faith is taking God at His Word. It is believing that what God says is true even though your human eyes are telling you that you are facing an impossible situation.
> JAN SILVIOUS

Bright Hope for Tomorrow

As the Scriptures say, "It is through faith that a righteous person has life."
Romans 1:17 NLT

You get faith from listening to and reading God's Word, and believing that it's true because you find proofs for your faith. Nurtured faith grows through the testing of trials and the hassles of living. Faith finds vitality from listening to lots of sermons and sitting under inspirational speakers. Faith develops when you conquer your fears, when you find the power to forgive, when you witness God heal a disease or a wounded relationship. Faith expands when you pray and keep a record of his answers.

Your faith invigorates when you reach out to people in need. Faith leads you to sick, hurting, mourning-over-sin kind of folks to give them hope.

Faith is trust in God that shows itself in actions, and it grows through spiritual disciples and personal interaction with the heavenly Father. Faith is a strong barrier against anything Satan can throw at you. Faith is the foundation for life. Faith is an attribute that can grow and that should develop. Practice one specific, stretching step of faith each day. Proclaim a positive faith statement. Pray believing that God will answer. Witness to someone who doesn't have faith.

words *to live by*

Things you might not know about *faith*:

❶ Human babies learn to trust their mothers through crying for their attention. The Moro reflex—that panicked, startled response that indicates the fear of falling—is shown by no other primate. From birth, baby chimpanzees cling to their mothers and hang on.

❶ The Shield of Faith Ministry in California is an outreach to firefighters, police officers, and their spouses based on Ephesians 6:16 as they are provided support and learn how to use their faith as a shield against the anger and frustrations due to their jobs.

The less I can depend on my intelligence and reasoning, the more I either have to live in fear because I don't know what's next or live in faith.
PATSY CLAIRMONT

We can't trust the God we don't know personally.
EUGENIA PRICE

The fundamental fact of existence is that this trust in God, this faith, is the firm foundation under everything that makes life worth living.
Hebrews 11:1
THE MESSAGE

God, increase my faith. I want to believe, to be assured with all my heart, that you can take care of any situation that faces me today. I trust you to do this for me.
Amen.

faith

He Is High and Exalted

fear of the Lord, noun.

1. the feeling of divine disapproval.
2. perceiving God as an enemy.
3. awe in the presence of a supreme power.
4. **Biblical:** worship of God's power and wisdom, holiness and grace.
5. **Personal:** reverence for God and his laws that leads to obedience.

fear of the Lord

The fear of the LORD is a fountain of life, so that one may avoid the snares of death.
Proverbs 14:27 NRSV

words *to live by*

What would it be like to peer into God's face, to stare him in the eyes? What would you expect to experience? Would it be a sweet moment or a terrifying encounter? Or something in between? One of the challenges in a relationship with almighty God is to envision him as he truly is, in all his awe-inspiring glory, but also to enjoy close communion with him. He is to be loved, but he is also to be feared. We should enjoy his presence and obey his commands.

In the Old Testament age the views of God were often accompanied with thunder, lightning flashes, and sounds like mighty trumpets. When Moses climbed down the mountain after talking with God, his people trembled and shook with dread and terror. They did not want God getting close to them. "Do not be afraid," Moses assured them. "God has come to test you, so that the fear of God will be with you to keep you from sinning" (Exodus 20:20).

To fear the Lord is to stand in awe of him for his high and exalted position. You show him proper reverence by obedience. By your actions, you award him the respect he is due. To fear the Lord is to worship him with your whole heart and to try to understand how to please him. It is realizing that you walk on holy ground.

Some fear the Lord because their view of him is that of a supreme, disapproving judge. But the opposite mistake can also be made, to treat him as a casual acquaintance or of no consequence in your daily challenges or choices.

The fear of the Lord keeps you honest as you hide nothing from him. You tell him the truth about everything, for you realize he knows it all anyway. That reverence prevents careless, flippant references about sacred things. It stirs up repentance. And consider the rewards—think of how many products are hawked to keep you young, yet the Bible says it is the fear of the Lord that is the fountain of life. That fear keeps you from harmful desires and life-threatening preferences.

Fear of the Lord is good and right. It's the beginning of wisdom. It's the secret of uprightness and true piety. It brings pleasure to God. But how do you grasp a proper fear of the Lord that produces heartfelt love and hope, as well as filial reverence, obedience, and worship?

> The word "reverence" speaks of that fear that is a godly fear, a proper fear. That fear is the rich convergence of awe in the presence of the eternal God.
> **ROBERT B. STRIMPLE**

71

...dness grace mercy love faith goodness truth freedom hope
orgiveness peace humble holiness obey repent perfect submit
serve fellowship comforter transformed noble character church

He Is High and Exalted

The fear of the
LORD is clean,
enduring forever;
the judgments of
the LORD are
true and righteous
altogether.

Psalm 19:9 NKJV

The fear of the Lord comes through God's Word. Study all God's attributes, such as his holiness and love, his faithfulness and righteous anger, his justice and mercy. Ponder his great and mighty acts, including the power it took to create this vast universe. Be conscious of the presence of God in everything you think and do. Get to know him. When you fear the Lord, you put him first—his plans, his purposes, his commands.

You want to reach out in love. You also want someone in your life to respect. The fear of the Lord arouses all those needs into one worthy being: the Lord of the universe. Reverence for him causes you to exalt him and obey him. You want to please him, as he has first place in all your decisions and affections. Proper fear of him gives him and his Word the highest regard.

words
to live by

Things you might not know about *fear of the Lord:*

❶ In Isaiah 11:2–3, the prophecy of the future Messiah included the information that "the Spirit of knowledge and of the fear of the Lord" would rest on him and that he would "delight in the fear of the Lord." To fear God is to delight in obedience.

❶ Phobia clinics report that one of the most ancient phobias is *zeusophobia*, an abnormal, persistent fear of God that prevents personal relationship.

I believe Jonah disobeyed because he had no righteous fear of God.
DAVID WILKERSON

Happy the soul that has been awed by a view of God's majesty.
ARTHUR W. PINK

Everything you were taught can be put into a few words: Respect and obey God! This is what life is all about.
Ecclesiastes 12:13 CEV

God, I love you. May holy fear of you penetrate my deepest being, that I will shun offensive things. Show me who you are that I will worship and reverence you with all my heart.
Amen.

fear of the Lord

A Beautiful Communion

fel·low·ship, noun.

1. a group of shared interests or experiences.
2. friendship; comradeship.
3. a social club.
4. **Biblical:** the body of Christ; the church.
5. **Personal:** a mutually ministering, serving gathering of believers.

fel·low·ship

We proclaim to you what we have seen and heard, so that you also may have fellowship with us. And our fellowship is with the Father and with his Son, Jesus Christ.

I John 1:3 NIV

Some women enjoy living alone with their own privacy, being able to do what they want when they want. But it's hard to be a hermit Christian. You need Christian friends to help you navigate the spiritual rocky bumps. Then there's the issue of using your gifts and talents and receiving back the sacraments of love and grace. None of this transpires if you don't enter the door to the Christian community and stake your claim as one of them. *Fellowship* means people—imperfect but important fellow travelers on the highway to heaven.

The Greek word for *fellowship* is *koinonia*, which also means "community," "communion," "joint participation." The Greek word *ekklesia* gives the idea of being called out together. In the fellowship of believers you share intimacy with a group of individuals with a common bond. In Christian fellowship, that bond is faith in Jesus Christ.

words
to live by

wôrds

The fellowship provides encouragement and support for each member, an environment for healthy spiritual growth, the chance to be trained in the art of love and service. The fellowship pulls its members into a circle of togetherness and caring. When troubles hit, the fellowship is there for you and you for them.

The Christian fellowship is distinctive from a social club or other community organization. It is a worshiping fellowship, a witnessing community. All its functions are oriented toward close friendship with and service for God. You are united by the joys of your salvation, your mutual love for your heavenly Father, dependence on the power of God's Spirit, the goal of making disciples for Jesus, and warfare against your common enemy, Satan. Your common purpose is to think of ways to "spur one another on toward love and good deeds" (Hebrews 10:24).

Christian fellowship encompasses singing, praying, sometimes eating together, the teaching of God's Word, and ordinances such as baptism and the Lord's Supper. Above all, God's presence is expected. Christian community has roots clear back to the Old Testament. No matter how new the fellowship, you've got connections to the ancient past. The New Testament records the birth of the church and the first instance of all believers being filled and controlled by the Holy Spirit.

It is a privilege to be welcomed into a fellowship by the community of believers in

Shun solitude. Eve got into trouble when she walked in the garden alone. I have my worst temptations when I am by myself. Undergird yourself with the fellowship of the church.
MARTIN LUTHER

75

ness grace mercy love faith goodness truth freedom hope
rgiveness peace humble holiness obey repent perfect submit
erve fellowship comforter transformed noble character church

A Beautiful Communion

Jesus Christ, the people of God. How do you get involved with a fellowship? First, you stay close to God on your own. Even in the midst of active ministry, Jesus withdrew to be alone with his Father. Second, you initiate your involvement and don't wait to be asked. Pay attention to announcements and join a smaller group for Bible study, prayer, or service. Let someone in ministry leadership know your interests and abilities. Look for needs that aren't being fulfilled. Share your own needs with a few others.

You help to grow a fellowship by your warmth, your handshake, your smile, by your showing your loving concern for each person who enters your group. You keep the fellowship spiritually healthy by your caring, by entering into the sorrows and joys, and by opening up your own home in hospitality.

They devoted themselves to the apostles' teaching and to the fellowship, to the breaking of bread and to prayer.
Acts 2:42 NIV

A fellowship of believers provides a community for being discipled, for mutual edification, and for learning how to love and serve. The best way to become an active member of a fellowship is to attend meetings that are announced, to take advantage of invitations to get involved. You get as much out of a fellowship as you're willing to give.

words
to live by

Things you might not know about *fellowship:*

❶ In the Bible, "the right hand of fellowship" meant clasping one right hand onto another right hand in a handshake. Paul was offered the right hand of fellowship after he submitted his teaching for examination by the apostles.

❶ More people exist on earth than ever before and enjoy the most sophisticated forms of communication, yet psychologists say loneliness remains a problem. Women, especially, are facing increasing loneliness because they're busier than ever, but less connected.

The human being is the only species that can't survive alone. The human being needs another human being.
LEONARD CAMMER

If two or three people come together in my name, I am there with them.
Matthew 18:20 NCV

Conversion to Jesus requires a new pattern of relationships. If every aspect of a person's life is to become truly Christian, that person needs to share life deeply with other Christians.
ROBERT SABATH

God, lead me to my appointed place in the fellowship of believers. I want to be in that gathering of your people to love and be loved, for your gospel's sake.
Amen.

fel·low·ship

A Healthy Pardon

for·give·ness, noun.

1. a debt cancelled.
2. a pardon granted.
3. an excusing of an offense.
4. **Biblical:** absolution of sin through confession and repentance.
5. **Personal:** letting go your right to be angry or vengeful.

for·give·ness

Phyllis considers herself a forgiving kind of woman. But what her sister did caused a great barrier between them. She betrayed Phyllis not once, but twice, and after Phyllis sternly warned her. In addition, her sister lied about it when confronted. Finally, Phyllis worked through to forgiveness when she realized how much she wanted God's spiritual purpose in both their lives.

Seven Hebrew and Greek words in the Bible cover the concept of forgiveness—five of them indicate "to cover" and "to pardon," also "to bear or take away," "to put away," "disregard." The Greek word *charizesthai* expresses the graciousness aspect of God's forgiveness. The more common word, *aphesis*, means to send away or to let go.

The Old Testament believer received forgiveness based on an animal sacrifice that covered over the sin. Forgiveness is possible now through the sacrifice of

> You must make allowance for each other's faults and forgive the person who offends you. Remember, the Lord forgave you, so you must forgive others.
> **Colossians 3:13** NLT

words
to live by

God's Son, which literally cancels out the sin. In the old system, sins weren't totally gone, in the strict sense. But through Jesus you can let it go, release it, get rid of every vestige of the offense. Like Jesus, you can forgive.

Even so, forgiveness presents complications. The human tendency is to placate a relationship enough to get by while still nursing private spite or venting public self-righteous rage. Surely, the reasoning goes, no one should condone outrageous behavior. You certainly don't want to minimize fair consequences or let a poor chooser off an immoral hook. Besides, almost everyone caught in an infraction offers excuses. Forgiveness might seem like telling them they couldn't help it, that they shouldn't be blamed for what they said or did.

However, human forgiveness is supposed to be similar to God's. He provides the means and the example. If certain conditions are fulfilled—confession and repentance—there is no limit to his offer of forgiveness. The main difference is that you might need to work through forgiveness before the one who hurt you asks for it—for your own sake. If you refuse to forgive, you suffer the backlash of bitterness and set in motion all kinds of unpredictable repercussions.

Forgiveness means you let it go. You release the negative emotions every time they threaten to consume you. You give up your right to prolong the grieving. You ease the impact of the shock and humiliation. You relinquish going over and over the memories that record the hurts. You get rid

Holding on to anger, resentment, and hurt only gives you tense muscles, a headache, and a sore jaw from clenching your teeth.
JOAN LUNDEN

A Healthy Pardon

of the reminders, the souvenirs of the details. You let go every temptation to seek revenge.

Forgiveness does not always happen quickly, nor does it necessarily change everything. It takes time to forgive bad hurts. You let it go by finding someone trustworthy to talk it all through, someone who will comfort you and at the same time issue exhortations about relinquishing your anger, liberating your need to nurse your grudge. Letting it go means you pray for good things to happen to the one who brought you such pain. You let go all your failure at forgiveness up to this moment and start again fresh. Forgiveness opens the possibility for divine miracles.

> Be kind to one another, tender-hearted, forgiving each other, just as God in Christ also has forgiven you.
> **Ephesians 4:32** NASB

Forgiveness is rarely easy, but you have a perfect role model—God's forgiveness of you. Forgiveness is choosing to let it all go—the emotional pain, the memories, the physical reminders. Letting go doesn't excuse the offense, but it frees you to be part of a godly solution, to prevent a widening circle of consequences. Forgiveness makes you more like Jesus.

words
to live by

Things you might not know about *forgiveness:*

❶ International Forgiveness Week was first observed by a gathering in Times Square, New York, in 1979. Usually set around Valentine's Day, it has expanded into a nondenominational, nonsectarian, nonpolitical movement.

❷ Amnesty applies to national and military affairs. It includes a full pardon of all offenders who come within its provisions. Oblivion signifies overlooking and virtually forgetting an offense, so that the offender stands before the law in all respects as if it had never been committed.

A Christian will find it cheaper to pardon than to resent. Forgiveness saves the expense of anger and the cost of hatred.
HANNAH MORE

Forgiveness is almost a selfish act because of its immense benefits to the one who forgives.
LAWANA BLACKWELL

Forgive us our debts, as we forgive our debtors.
Matthew 6:12 NKJV

God, I need your help. Fill me with the will to forgive and the insight for how to make it work whenever I meet with that person again. Do your miracle of love through me. Amen.

for·give·ness

A Chosen Communication

God's Word, noun.

1. the Bible.
2. the sacred volume of Christians.
3. the books of the Old and New Testament, sometimes including the Apocrypha.
4. **Biblical:** the Holy Spirit–breathed and inspired words from God to all humankind.
5. **Personal:** God's chosen channel of speaking to you.

God's Word

Everything in the Scriptures is God's Word. All of it is useful for teaching and helping people and for correcting them and showing them how to live. The Scriptures train God's servants to do all kinds of good deeds.

2 Timothy 3:16–17
CEV

What is the vital issue in your life? Security? God's Word tells you the source. Contentment? God's Word tell you how to find it. Your family? God's Word instructs you how to enjoy one another, how to get along. Your job? God's Word gives you a proper perspective on choosing careers and work habits. Confused about what is truth and what isn't? You can sort it all out through God's Word.

God's Word is the completed canon of Scripture—the Old Testament as designated by the Jews and the New Testament accepted by Christians as authoritative, as opposed to certain noncanonical epistles and other religious writings produced and circulated in biblical times. God's Word is composed of those writings characterized as inspired by God and other elements outlined in 1 Timothy 3:16–17.

God's Word is what God has to say

words
to live by

about humans, about himself, about redemption, about eternity. It is God's Word to you. The message focuses on Jesus. Jesus' resurrection proved the validity of all God's Word, and even the betrayal of Jesus by Judas was a fulfillment of the prophecies of God's Word. God's Word reveals facts about God's character, likes and dislikes, and his works that you could not learn from any other source. The Bible tells you how to know God, how to do relationships, how to find a God-honoring purpose. Without God's Word, you would never know about the salvation that Jesus made possible. The Bible is your book of life.

Someone may challenge you that the Bible is the equivalent of any spiritual-sounding book. In the debater's mind, anything written or said that sounds like truth is a sacred writing. Other books certainly can be considered authoritative in their field and, therefore, the bible of that area of limited knowledge. But only the Christian Bible is God's Word and true for any century, any culture, any circumstance. It will always be valid and relevant.

To get the fullest benefit for your life from God's Word, let it penetrate not only your mind but your heart as well. Allow its principles of wisdom to affect every choice, every relationship. Give God's Word the attention it deserves, and it will dwell in you, make its home in you, completely fill you. Sing its psalms. Study its history. Share its proverbs with friends and neighbors.

It helps to keep in mind that the Bible is God's love letters to you. . . . God's love letters to you are full of messages. They say, "This is how much I love you."
STORMIE OMARTIAN

grace mercy love faith goodness truth freedom hope
rgiveness peace humble holiness obey repent perfect submit
serve fellowship comforter transformed noble character church

A Chosen Communication

Always remember what is written in the Book of the Teachings. Study it day and night to be sure to obey everything that is written there. If you do this, you will be wise and successful in everything.

Joshua 1:8 NCV

Find a quiet place and read a whole book or several chapters of the Bible. To keep your mind from wandering, journal while you read. Note passages that strike you as more personal. Explain how they apply to you. Jot notes in the margins. Use a highlighter on especially pertinent passages. Listen to God's Word on a CD while you walk, drive, or clean house. Find a one-year program that assigns a portion every day. Do a topical study on a subject of special interest or on an issue you're facing. Join an organized Bible study group. God's Word can be studied, meditated upon, and proved by putting it into practice. Whenever you need comfort or direction from God, God's Word will speak to you.

🔒

The Word of God teaches everything you need to know about God, Jesus, and how to live the Christian life. God's Word sustains your spiritual life and is your lifeline to a relationship with God. God's Word is the truth against which all other knowledge is measured. God communicates with you in a very personal way through the pages of this inspired book.

words
to live by

Things you might not know about *God's Word:*

❶ A Gallup Poll reported "occasional" Bible readers in America fell from 79 percent in the 1980s to 59 percent in 2001. A Barna survey of Christians found that 22 percent thought there is a book of Thomas in the Bible; 13 percent did not know.

❶ Moses wrote the most books in the Old Testament—the first five, called the Pentateuch. The apostle Paul wrote over half the New Testament—fourteen books, which include letters to various churches.

We must each do whatever it takes to become men and women who know the Bible book-by-book, and who live in accordance to the whole counsel of God.
KAY ARTHUR

I realized long ago that I have nothing to give anyone unless it is a word from God. And sometimes I have to get away from the rat race and find that word.
JILL BRISCOE

Do not merely listen to the word, and so deceive yourselves. Do what it says.
James 1:22 NIV

God, thank you that I possess a copy of your precious book. Help me understand what you want me to know and how to apply your truth to my life.
Amen.

God's Word

The Avoidable Burden

guilt, noun.

1. responsibility for an offense.
2. blame.
3. the legal status of having broken the law.
4. **Biblical:** a condition incurred by a sin against God.
5. **Personal:** chagrin for a shameful act committed against God or another person.

guilt

My friends, the blood of Jesus gives us courage to enter the most holy place by a new way that leads to life! And this way takes us through the curtain that is Christ himself.
Hebrews 10:19–20
CEV

An inner uneasiness gnaws at your mind. You're sad and depressed. Your stomach churns. You can't sleep, and you're not hungry. You wonder if you should go to the doctor for a checkup or go to see a counselor. Then you remember what you did. You recall the choices you made and what will happen if anyone finds out. You finally recognize your condition as guilt.

It is God who exposes guilt. His Spirit uncovers sin. *Guilt* is the feeling of fear of exposure, the dread of consequences, the despair of failing the Lord, yourself, and others. The common misconception is that once you deal with your sin, your guilt will go. Instead, the residue of guilt hangs on, despite the amazing promise of God that "If we confess our sins, he is faithful and just and will forgive us our sins and purify us from all unrighteousness" (1 John 1:9). That should be enough to remove the hugest weight from

words
to live by

any confessing heart. Instead of binding you, bogging you down, guilt should motivate you to action.

The guilty have a tendency to hide, rather than open the spirit to God, to his correction and forgiveness. But human effort alone can't free you from the sense of guilt. It took a touch from the Lord to take away Isaiah's guilt. Isaiah saw God on his throne and felt the full force of the guilt of his sins. "My doom is sealed," he said. Then one of God's angels touched his lips and pronounced him not guilty. Isaiah was free of his burden, and he was free to wholeheartedly serve the Lord.

As you deal with your guilt, learn from it. Assess your behavior patterns and make some corrections. Determine that you never want to go through this again. Take steps to make sure that you will avoid situations that might cause you to be a repeat offender. It's better to do the hard work of prevention of sin rather than to agonize to overcome guilt. Try to make amends for any physical, emotional, or spiritual damage you've caused someone.

Listen to God's voice through the Scriptures. Find verses that help you deal with guilt (such as Hebrews 10:22) and tape them to your computer, your bathroom mirror, and on the tablet of your heart. Write a poem, a song, a letter of repentance and thanksgiving to God, just as David did in Psalm 51. Stand on the truth of what God says, not on how you feel. Guilt feelings

No work of love will flourish out of guilt, fear, or hollowness of heart, just as no valid plans for the future can be made by those who have no capacity for living now.
ALAN WATTS

The Avoidable Burden

Let us draw near to God with a sincere heart in full assurance of faith, having our hearts sprinkled to cleanse us from a guilty conscience and having our bodies washed with pure water.
Hebrews 10:22 NIV

fade away when you proclaim God's forgiveness of you daily and believe it. Trust and believe. Daily ask to be filled with God's Spirit. Let him free you from condemnation.

It is by the power of Jesus' name and his sinless perfection that God purifies your heart and conscience and you dare draw near to God without guilt. Just like a shower cleans your body, his blood cleanses your soul. Let God touch you, fill you with himself, give you peace by the imputed gift of his purity.

Guilt is remorse and awareness that you've done something wrong. God forgives you when you confess and repent, but the feelings of guilt may linger. Instead of berating yourself for having these feelings, use them for positive action. Change your habits that lead to sin. But you can't get rid of guilt on your own. You find God's help by poring over his Word, talking to him, and releasing the memories of the past.

words
to live by

etcetera . . .

Things you might not know about *guilt:*

❶ Counselors note that persons who fear success often suffer from guilt. Most guilt-ridden persons know how to fail, but not how to succeed. Opportunities immobilize them. They put up guilt smokescreens to avoid taking the steps that would possibly bring them prosperity.

❶ Court defendants can plead guilty without admitting guilt by entering Alford and *nolo contendere* pleas. Some argue that these pleas risk not only convicting innocent defendants, but also impede the reform and condemnation of guilty defendants. One might call them guilty-but-not-guilty pleas.

One key to successful relationships is learning to say "no" without guilt, so that you can say "yes" without resentment.
BILL CRAWFORD

It is rather hard and certainly depressing to admit guilt and to repent.
HANNAH ARENDT

The Spirit of life in Christ, like a strong wind, has magnificently cleared the air, freeing you from a fated lifetime of brutal tyranny at the hands of sin and death.
Romans 8:2
THE MESSAGE

God, I want to be completely free to serve you with all my heart. I open my life to you. Correct me, cleanse me, forgive me. Show me how to walk humbly. Amen.

...ness grace mercy love faith goodness truth freedom hope
orgiveness peace humble holiness obey repent perfect submit
serve fellowship comforter transformed noble character church

The Search for Restoration

heal·ing, noun.

1. the recovery of something lost or impaired.
2. the curing of wellness or health.
3. the remedying of an illness.
4. **Biblical:** an act that God performs on ill or broken minds, bodies, or broken relationships.
5. **Personal:** the restoration of spiritual, emotional, or physical wholeness.

heal·ing

Heal me, O LORD, and I will be healed; save me and I will be saved, for you are the one I praise.
Jeremiah 17:14 NIV

words
to live by

A woman who had been bleeding for twelve years spent all her money going to numerous doctors but had only gotten worse. She heard about Jesus and how he had healed so many kinds of diseases. A seed of faith had been planted. An idea developed: she had to get to Jesus. She pushed through the crowds that were pressed around him, weak as she was, and reached out to touch him. Her bleeding stopped.

The Greek word for healing is *therapeuo* and signifies "to serve as an attendant." Healing is the ministry of caring for the sick in order to treat, to cure, to restore to health. Healing was a part of Jesus' everyday ministry. His disciples were ministers of healing by faith in his name. Healing in the Bible applies to physical, emotional, and spiritual wholeness and refers to being saved from disease and sin and its effects. You, too, can plead to God for healing.

To be restored to spiritual health requires God's grace and forgiveness. His discipline in your life is meant to lead to repentance and healing. Returning to God can be the first step in both physical and spiritual healing.

Most doctors understand that they are practitioners to help the body heal itself. When you are injured, a natural healing process begins at once to restore soundness. In an infected wound, an emergency blood supply rushes white cells and other agents of repair to the area. But the agent of that healing is the power of God. When you recover from any wound or disease, it is God who restores you.

Healing is restoring a person to what they had before and lost. Healing is setting something right—whether mending broken bones or a broken relationship or freeing a troubled mind. Healing is finding a remedy, reconciling a difference, regaining one's strength. You can ask God for healing. You can pray with faith that God will heal you, if doing so will bring him glory and further your eternal welfare. Allow God to use whatever means he chooses to restore you.

Healing happens faster with cooperation. You apply all you know to help bring it about. Perhaps you need lots of rest. Or you must work to strengthen your

When we honestly ask ourselves which person in our lives means the most to us, we often find that it is those who, instead of giving advice, solutions, or cures, have chosen rather to share our pain and touch our wounds with a warm and tender hand.
HENRI NOUWEN

ness grace mercy love faith goodness truth freedom hope
orgiveness peace humble holiness obey repent perfect submit
serve fellowship comforter transformed noble character church

> Strengthen the hands which hang down, and the feeble knees, and make straight paths for your feet, so that what is lame may not be dislocated, but rather be healed.
> **Hebrews 12:12–13**
> NKJV

muscles. Or you get out and exercise. Or eat right. A song can bring healing. So can kind words. Healing may require getting rid of self-defeating thoughts or confessing your sins. Do everything you can to make peace with yourself, your neighbor, and with God. However, doing everything right doesn't guarantee healing, but it does help to restore your attitude and to be all you can be in the midst of your limitations.

Some genetic diseases happen simply because you live in a fallen world. Some sexually transmitted ailments are caused by sin. Some mental illnesses are caused by Satan. All sickness can be healed by God. He is the restorer of soul, mind, and body, and he will heal you completely some day. In heaven you are more than restored; you are completely made into a new being.

words to live by

Healing is being restored to health or soundness. The desire for healing can set you on a search for God and his power. God does heal. He has various means of restoring his children. Sometimes he uses doctors. He also wants your cooperation with good health practices. But all healing comes from God.

etcetera . . .

Things you might not know about *healing:*

❶ The Book of Luke was written from a doctor's perspective. Luke, a physician, made references to healing fifteen different times and offers a bit more medical detail.

❶ In a telephone poll of 1,004 adult Americans taken for TIME/CNN, 82 percent said they believed in the healing power of personal prayer; 73 percent said praying for someone else can help cure their illness; 77 percent said God sometimes intervenes to cure people who have a serious illness.

With the gift of listening comes the gift of healing.
CATHERINE DE HUECK

Our prayers should be for a sound mind in a healthy body.
JUVENAL

I will give you back your health and heal your wounds, says the LORD.
Jeremiah 30:17 NLT

God, many around me are sick and weary and in need of your healing touch. Restore those I bring to you by name. Let their journeys to health bring them close to you. Amen.

heal·ing

The Secret Places

heart, noun.

1. one's innermost being.
2. the center of secret thoughts and emotions.
3. the capacity for love and affection.
4. **Biblical:** the base of human moral action.
5. **Personal:** the real you that's so secret only God can know it.

heart

Search me, O God, and know my heart; test me and know my anxious thoughts. See if there is any offensive way in me, and lead me in the way everlasting.
Psalm 139:23–24 NIV

It's a hollow muscle in the middle of your chest that pumps blood around your body. The more popular image depicts it as a red, lacy valentine that transports romantic messages. The Bible portrays it in a much different way.

The Hebrew word *leb* or *lebab* stands for "heart," "mind," "midst." It may refer to the physical body organ or to "the inner part or middle of a thing." It is used of the inner part of a person, the hidden part of your personality. Human depravity resides in the heart. Sin pulsates from there. By invitation, it's where God's Spirit lives. It's the center of conscience, character, and all that you do, and only God can see it.

In spite of David's sins, God was impressed with him. God said David was "a man after my own heart; he will do everything I want him to do." David's overall spiritual focus was right.

words
to live by

The heart comprises all your thoughts, desires, words, and actions that flow from deep within you. It is hard to understand your own heart. Only God does. The heart is what causes you grief. It is the spring and the source of your motives and affections. Fickle, erratic behavior and every kind of sin originates in the heart. To know your heart is to know you. To give your heart is to share the most important part of you. What to do with your heart can be summed up this way: guard it against evil and store good things in it.

It's important to guard your heart because the seeds of sin start there. Be alert to any suspicious activity. Keep your heart from being weighed down by anxiety. Avoid excessive, obsessive longings for anything or anyone in this world, except God alone. When your heart is full of sorrow or anguish or unrestrained, disorderly affections, give it to him. In fact, give him your heart the first thing each morning.

You can choose the focus of your heart. Try to keep your heart "undivided"—stay single-minded, concentrating on devotion to God and doing his will. Your heart stays guarded when you keep it behind the protective guardrail of God's Word. You can practice disciplines of the mind to protect your heart from hardness and evil by careful attention to the Scriptures. Ask God to inspect your heart, to search all its crevices, then ask him to

God performed surgery on my friend, open heart surgery. He made a bypass of love around an artery congested with hate.
ANNA BELLE LAUGHBAUM

ness grace mercy love faith goodness truth freedom hope
orgiveness peace humble holiness obey repent perfect submit
serve fellowship comforter transformed noble character church

The Secret Places

cleanse it until it pleases him. When necessary, God will do spiritual surgery on your heart. He can even give you a fresh, new one if the old one is stony hard.

What you put in your heart reveals itself sooner or later in words and actions. Therefore, store good things in your heart. Store up love for God. Store up love for your neighbor that is pure and sincere. Store up God's Word. Store up all the joys you can. Store up forgiveness. Store up spiritual knowledge and apply it to wisdom. Store up understanding of God and his ways. Store up a well full of praise and thanksgiving.

Above all else, guard your heart, for it is the wellspring of life.
Proverbs 4:23 NIV

The heart is the seat of your personality and the spring for all your words and actions. Give your heart to God before you give it to anyone else or it will be divided and unfocused spiritually. The most important things you can do for your heart: guard it from evil and store up good things in it. And every day, give your heart to God.

words
to live by

etcetera . . .

Things you might not know about *heart*:

❶ The term *heartstrings* developed from the notions of anatomy held before the seventeenth century that sinews and tendons braced and sustained the physical heart. In time that became a symbol of the deepest feelings or affections.

❶ Angioplasty balloons used for heart surgery must withstand air pressure about eight times greater than the pressure in the typical automobile tire, but they have to be thin enough to inflate inside an artery of the heart, which is at largest only a third the size of an ink pen.

The tongue responds to the heart condition of its owner.
LINDA BANZ

In the presence of melted hearts wrongs are forgiven and hurt hearts healed.
DORIS M. MCDOWELL

I will behave myself wisely in a perfect way. I will walk within my house with a perfect heart.
Psalm 101:2 KJV

God, search my heart and purify it from everything that distracts me from you and your will for my life. I want a heart like yours. Amen.

heart

ho·li·ness, noun.

1. perfection; spiritual purity.
2. moral excellence.
3. an attribute belonging only to God.
4. *Biblical:* the state of sanctification.
5. *Personal:* being more like Jesus.

ho · li · ness

Let's make a clean break with everything that defiles or distracts us, both within and without. Let's make our entire lives fit and holy temples for the worship of God.

2 Corinthians 7:1
THE MESSAGE

Holiness is a set-you-on-a-pedestal type word for the average woman. It conjures up visions of cathedrals with stained-glass windows parading a gallery of saints in white robes. Surely heroines for the faith never went mall shopping when they should have cleaned house or ever got angry enough to scream and throw things or gave into temptation. Surely holiness can only happen for missionaries or martyrs.

Yet, holiness is a result of the disciplines of trying to be like Jesus as you face your ordinary duties and daily kinds of struggles.

Holiness is a heart set on God in everything you do. It's serving the needs of other people out of gratitude for what God has done for you. It's a peaceful, quiet lifestyle. Holiness is being set apart by God to be his child and to do his work, his way. That perspective gets your eyes on Jesus and perfecting holiness. You try

words
to live by

harder to obey God when you realize he's your heavenly Father and you want to please him. Holiness is perfection of character, found in God and Jesus only, and it is trying to be like Jesus. Holiness is loving God with all your heart, soul, and mind. Holiness is allowing thanksgiving to crowd out the impurities in your life, knowing you owe everything you are to God's grace. It is being wholly intent on doing God's will and on being joined to Jesus Christ to share his nature and consent for him to be your boss. Holiness is wholeness, completeness, maturity, a finishing of what has been started in your life.

Jesus' death for your sins produced holiness for you forever, but that holiness won't be seen in its completeness until you go to heaven. In the meanwhile, you strive to show it more and more. As you grow as God's child in holiness, you will exhibit his traits and become more comfortable getting close to Jesus. The Greek word for *saint, hagios,* is the same as the word for *holy.* If you believe in and follow Jesus, you have the right to be called a saint, that is, one of the holy ones. You have been called by God to be set aside by him for some special purpose.

Holiness is different from legalism. Legalism is interpreting Scripture for your life, then forcing it as an absolute rule for every believer. For instance, the Bible says to treat your body like a holy temple. One personal interpretation might be to go on a diet to lose weight. Legalism would say, "Everybody has to go on a diet of vegetables and water in order to be spiritual." Holiness

When we draw upon the power of Jesus' name, holiness becomes a throbbing, pulsating connection with the divine dynamo.
W. T. PURKISER

ness grace mercy love faith goodness truth freedom hope
rgiveness peace humble holiness obey repent perfect submit
erve fellowship comforter transformed noble character church

More Like Jesus

Now that you are obedient children of God do not live as you did in the past. . . . Be holy in all you do, just as God, the One who called you, is holy.

I Peter 1:14–15 NCV

is also different from innocence. To be innocent is to never have false motives, never blow up, never sin. Holiness acknowledges and confesses sin as quickly as possible. Holiness sets boundaries to help keep you out of trouble and has an increased sensitivity to sin. Holiness is showing your love and reverence for God by offering your heart, mind, and body to him. Jesus in you is your holiness.

🔒

God is holy and makes you holy by Jesus, his Son, trading his life for your sins. Holiness is God living his life through you. Holiness is wholeness, God completing his work in you by accomplishing a special spiritual purpose. Holiness is being wholly his. Set your heart to please and obey God out of gratitude and love.

words
to live by

Things you might not know about *holiness:*

❶ The Greek word for "saint," *hagios,* is the same as the word for "holy." A saint is one who is set aside for God's purpose—and that includes every Christian.

❶ John Wesley's theology of Christian perfection was the inspiration for the holiness movement and Methodism after the Civil War. Wesley believed sin could be eradicated in an instant moment of grace to produce the perfection of love that triumphs over sinful desires and selfish motives.

God's road home is the highway of holiness. On it there are no longer the hazards of hypocrisy, jealousy, or resentment.
REBA FITZ

Living a holy life makes us the light that shines in the increasing darkness of our day.
RUTH E. VAN REKEN

You are God's children. He sent Christ Jesus to save us and to make us wise, acceptable, and holy.
1 Corinthians 1:30 CEV

God, help me not to expect of others a perfection that I could never achieve myself. Let me see you in them and help them see you in me. In that way, we are all perfect. Amen.

h·o·l·i·n·e·s·s

ress grace mercy love faith goodness truth wisdom hope
rgiveness peace humble holiness obey repent perfect submit
erve fellowship comforter transformed noble character church

The Quiet Strength

hum·ble, adjective.

1. showing deferential respect.
2. modest and meek.
3. aware of one's faults.
4. **Biblical:** submissive to the ruling hand of God in all the affairs of your life.
5. **Personal:** not demanding recognition or reprisal.

h u m · b l e

Your attitude should be the same as that of Christ Jesus: . . . being found in appearance as a man, he humbled himself and became obedient to death—even death on a cross!
Philippians 2:5, 8 NIV

Stella felt fat and couldn't keep her mind off her weight. Her friends told her she was beautiful. A co-worker told her bluntly she was too skinny. Stella was shocked when her mother told her she was getting too prideful. Stella truly thought she was as humble as she could get.

The Greek word for *humble, tapeinos,* is always used in a positive sense in God's Word, even though the word denotes "brought low" or "of low degree." God exalts the humble, and believers are urged to show deference to those of low estate: Paul received comfort from Titus as one who was cast down. Those in humble circumstances are exhorted to take pride in their high position. God esteems those who are humble; he lifts them up and empowers them for service.

Abigail, wife of Nabal, a very wealthy man, knew David was angry enough at her husband's insults to kill. She could

words
to live by

run. She could try to shame David out of his revenge. Or she could be more understanding and creative. She prepared food and presents for David and his men and summoned great courage to tactfully, humbly bow before his prideful wrath. She didn't make a big show to either man about what she had done. She protected their dignity. Yet her gentle strength averted a dire disaster for them both. There can be power in being humble.

Being humble is seeing yourself in relation to God and others with your eyes wide open. It is depending on God's strength to forgive slights and restrain revenge, and it is delighted when others get praised and sincerely joins in the applause. Being humble is an opportunity to look for ways to make others look good. When an expected honor passes the humble by, they release it to God, knowing he's the only audience to be pleased. The humble get their attention off themselves and onto others.

True humility differs from the traditional view that to be humble is to be wimpy and beaten down and to let everyone walk all over you. Humility walks with gentle assurance that God will avenge. Humility is spirited participation from the sidelines but will stroll to center stage when needed. Humility waits for God's direction before speaking out and charging forward. Humility never indulges self-abasement because it's putting the self down in order to get attention.

If we're looking for humility . . . we gaze at God. More to the point, at Christ. No, even more humbling, we drag ourselves to the cross. Pride is suffocated at the cross.
JONI EARECKSON TADA

...ness grace mercy love faith goodness truth freedom hope
...rgiveness peace humble holiness obey repent perfect submit
...erve fellowship comforter transformed noble character church

The Quiet Strength

Take my yoke upon you. Let me teach you, because I am humble and gentle, and you will find rest for your souls.
Matthew 11:29 NLT

How do you get humility, the honest-to-goodness real kind? By desiring it. By making it the matter of constant prayer. By practicing it in the tough people challenges you face. Many of the tests of life come to teach you humility.

You become humble by taking the lower place at the table of life and being content. You gain humility by paying attention to the immensity of the universe and how small your place is in it. Humility finds unobtrusive, acceptable ways to wash the feet of others. To be humble is to bow before your place in life as a privileged position, realizing that God might lift you up from there anytime he wants.

●

Humility is controlled strength. The humble praise God when others are preferred in some way. The humble see themselves clearly in relationship to God and other people, and they delight in applauding others. They restrain their anger and urge for revenge and instead wait on God to lift them up when the timing's just right.

words
to live by

etcetera . . .

Things you might not know about *humble:*

❶ Ben Franklin made a personal list of virtues and proudly showed it to his Quaker friend, who mentioned one he'd left out: humility. It's no wonder, the friend said as he cited many examples of Franklin's pride. Franklin added humility to his list but never perfected the virtue.

❶ Greek philosophers looked down on humility. In the classical Greek writings, humility was despised as a servile trait. Biblical teaching elevated humility to a noble place.

Humility is strong—not bold; quiet—not speechless; sure—not arrogant.
ESTELLE SMITH

Humility is not a thing that will come of itself, but must be made the object of special desire, prayer, faith, and practice.
ANDREW MURRAY

Don't brag about yourself—let others praise you.
Proverbs 27:2 CEV

God, I praise you for the example of Jesus, humble and gentle of heart, yet not timid to step into the fray. Help me know my place and my part.
Amen.

h u m · b l e

A Glorious Gladness

joy, noun.

1. a feeling of happiness because of good fortune or well-being.
2. relief from pain or evil.
3. that which inspires gladness.
4. **Biblical:** the rapture of possessing the gift of salvation.
5. **Personal:** the complete happiness of knowing Jesus.

joy

You will go out with joy and be led out in peace. The mountains and hills will burst into song before you, and all the trees in the fields will clap their hands.
Isaiah 55:12 NCV

There're times when you need to laugh. It breaks the mood of melancholy or anxiety. Wholesome laughter makes a bond that molds friendship between two humans. Healthy things happen when you laugh together. Knowing how to laugh can jump-start joy.

The Greek word *chara* means "joy," "delight." It's akin to *chairo*, "to rejoice." Gaining spiritual knowledge is reason enough to rejoice, to celebrate before God. The Bible says that joy comes from trusting God and the hope he gives. Joy grows directly in proportion to the size and growth of your faith. Your joy as a Christian bubbles out of knowing Jesus. And you experience the joy of Jesus through the inner presence and power of God's Spirit. You learn to trust his love and power to see you through whatever life brings. In fact, trials and sorrows faced with the Lord enlarge your capacity for joy.

words
to live by

Paul and Silas were falsely accused, severely flogged, and thrown into prison with their feet in stocks. Then, the Bible records, "About midnight Paul and Silas were praying and singing hymns to God, and the other prisoners were listening to them" (Acts 16:25 NIV). Another time when the apostles were flogged, they rejoiced because "God had counted them worthy to suffer dishonor for the name of Jesus" (Acts 5:41 NLT).

Jesus' coming to earth infused this planet with an unlimited resource for joy. God himself is your ultimate joy as you boast, glory, and exult in him. Joy comes easily in spurts, such as the momentary, superficial joy that erupts at occasions like sporting events, when your team wins. But there aren't that many really great moments that deserve such a response. Few women can drum up fizzy, fuzzy feelings on demand. You have this perception that as a woman who knows Christ you should be smiling all the time. You should never have a down day. Your personality should be effervescent. And you might feel like a fool dancing in the streets for no reason, with all that's going on in the world and around you. Yet, the Bible commands you to rejoice in the Lord always. Joy should be possible in the commonplace, in the humdrum of the ordinary. The source of your joy is the secret.

Joy comes by your starting the day in fellowship with him. You receive joy from the insights of God's Word, and joy continues as you give thanks to God in everything that happens and as you do each activity. Joy

> The glory and grace of Jesus is that he is, and always will be, indestructibly happy.
> JOHN PIPER

ness grace mercy love faith goodness truth freedom hope
rgiveness peace humble holiness obey repent perfect submit
erve fellowship comforter transformed noble character church

A Glorious Gladness

May the God of hope fill you with all joy and peace in believing, that you may abound in hope by the power of the Holy Spirit.
Romans 15:13 NKJV

stays constant when you flee to God for safety when trouble comes, and you find him near. His closeness is sensed in his proofs of protection and in his surrounding you with his favor and quiet miracles.

You can bring about your own joy by asking God for the desire of your heart. Joy also comes through the people God brings into your life—you never know when an extra-plus catalyst for joy is just around the corner: a visit with a cheerful friend or good news.

Joy is less of a feeling and more of a fact. As you walk with Jesus through your day, joy becomes a by-product of fellowship with him through the Holy Spirit. God's kind of joy exists even in the midst of afflictions and sorrow. In fact, your capacity for joy increases as you trust in him through life's trials.

words
to live by

Things you might not know about *joy*:

❶ *Pollyanna* is a synonym for someone who is always happy. Pollyanna was the heroine of the popular novel of the same name by Eleanor Hodgman Porter (1868–1920). She played the "glad game" and brought joy to everyone she met.

❶ Psychologists enumerate the advantages of the experience of joy: Joy stimulates the immune system, increases energy, enhances mental ability, fosters creativity, and maximizes one's ability to experience life. Joy is an all-around health and productivity enhancer.

When we hold back any area of our lives from God, we subject our joy to whims of circumstances.
STACEY S. PADRICK

Real joy comes only as we love the Lord with all our heart, soul and mind. He is the reason we keep on keeping on.
SHELLY ESSER

These things have I [Jesus] spoken unto you, that my joy might remain in you, and that your joy might be full.
John 15:11 KJV

joy

God, how I enjoy your presence. Thank you for the many spiritual blessings you've brought to my life. I accept and receive the joy you provide. Amen.

jus·tice, noun.

1. administration of the law.
2. honor and fairness.
3. adherence to truth and facts.
4. **Biblical:** receiving from the Lord what your sin deserves.
5. **Personal:** fitting the right and fair reward or punishment to the act committed.

jus·tice

Getting Their Just Deserts

"It's not fair." Children whine it about the sharing of treats. Teens yell it over curfews and homework. You think it more often than you used to, as you see the news and read your tax returns. You want to get some breaks, and lawbreakers and cheaters to get what they deserve. You want evildoers to face the consequences of their actions. But it seems so many work the system for leniency or get away scot-free. Your heart cries for justice.

Let justice roll on like a river, right-eousness like a never-failing stream!
Amos 5:24 NIV

The Hebrew word *mishpat* means "justice"—the execution of judgment. It involves the act of deciding a case, a procedure of litigation before judges, a decision in law. The Greek for *justice* is *dike*, "what is right" or "a judicial hearing," "the execution of a sentence" or "punishment." In a broad sense, justice brings the offender to a state of righteousness, the condition acceptable to God. To get to justice requires integrity, purity, correct thinking, feeling, and acting on the part of

words
to live by

the judge. Justice is God's design: he wants the world ruled in justice.

By justice, God flooded the earth and all was destroyed, except Noah and his family. By justice, he destroyed Sodom and Gomorrah for their many sins. By justice, God called his people out from slavery in the oppressive Egyptian regime in order to establish a new society of freedom in the Promised Land.

When Jesus asked the Father if there could be some other way than taking the full brunt of the sins of the world upon his own being through crucifixion on the cross, he received only silence. There was no other way for God's justice, as well as his grace and mercy, to take place. In the future, one of Jesus' roles is to bring about final, ultimate justice on this earth.

Human nature seeks vengeance rather than justice. In the old west, when towns were being established quicker than judges and marshals could be installed, groups organized into vigilantes who took the law into their hands. The problem was that often there was no objective accountability. Revenge can come too naturally. Besides, the accused is considered innocent until proven guilty. Vigilantes would hang the accused before giving them a trial. Justice wars against vengeance. God instituted governments and officials to maintain order, and laws help restrain evil. God's Word provides an infallible guide to justice.

> No attribute of God is in conflict with another. His compassion flows out of his goodness, and goodness without justice is not goodness.
> **A. W. TOZER**

ss grace mercy love faith goodness truth freedom hope
rgiveness peace humble holiness obey repent perfect submit
erve fellowship comforter transformed noble character church

Getting Their Just Deserts

Satisfaction and contentment come to those who do the work of justice. When you do justice, you reflect God's own nature. You can do justice by righting some wrong in your family, your job, or your community. Prayer is a means of bringing justice to your world. Prayer gives you direct contact with the Judge of all the earth. Pray for your country's leaders to be wise and just.

A study of God's justice can make you very uncomfortable because you soon realize that everyone is an evildoer in God's sight. That's when you cry out for his mercy too. The good news is, mercy is very much a part of God's justice. And all final justice on this earth will come from his hands.

Righteousness and justice are the foundations of your throne. Mercy and truth stand in front of you.
Psalm 89:14
GOD'S WORD

🔒

Justice is fair judgment in deciding a case that exacts the perfect punishment or award. Justice requires objective analysis, critical thinking, and accountability. Justice is an attribute of God and can be an attribute of humans when they work through established governments and law. Stand up for justice, whenever you can, when things around you aren't right.

words
to live by

etcetera . . .

Things you might not know about *justice:*

❶ Arguments about justice in punishment for lawbreakers usually center on what works. Some professionals contend that prisons deter; other professionals argue that prisons rehabilitate. Both have contributed to the huge prison-building boom. The prison population has doubled in the past decade.

❶ The Lady of Justice symbol comes from Greek, Roman, and Egyptian sources. She sometimes wears a blindfold and sometimes holds a sword and scales. She is usually draped in flowing robes. She stands for fair and equal administration of the law, without corruption, avarice, prejudice, or favor.

Earthly power doth then show likest God's, when mercy seasons justice.
WILLIAM SHAKESPEARE

While we all hope for peace it shouldn't be peace at any cost but peace based on principle, on justice.
CORAZON AQUINO

Criminals don't know what justice means, but all who respect the LORD understand it completely.
Proverbs 28:5 CEV

God, help me know when I can work to bring justice to someone around me. Help me always to be fair. Thank you for showing your mercy and grace to me.
Amen.

jus·tice

His Rich Resources

knowl·edge, noun.

1. the sum or range of what is known.
2. specific data about a subject or someone.
3. what is gained by schooling and study.
4. **Biblical:** discernment and understanding that leads to eternal life.
5. **Personal:** information that helps you respond to life's circumstances God's way.

knowl·edge

The heavens declare the glory of God, and the sky displays what his hands have made. One day tells a story to the next. One night shares knowledge with the next.
Psalm 19:1–2
GOD'S WORD

words
to live by

It's human to want knowledge, to want to know things. A Polar Lander is sent from Cape Canaveral to land on Mars with all kinds of probing equipment. Even a microphone is included, to pick up Martian sounds, if any. Lots of expense and effort is expended to examine data and to send back photos of the red planet. It's hoped that information received will help determine whether Mars ever flowed with water. Polar Lander's mission is one more step in the long, exciting journey to gain knowledge.

The Hebrew word *yada* stands for *knowledge*, "to know." In the Greek, *ginosko* indicates "to be taking in knowledge," "to come to know," "to recognize or understand," or "to understand completely," with emphasis on knowledge of God and his truth. Such knowledge is not obtained by intellectual effort, experience, or observation, but through insight of the

Holy Spirit, by those who "know" Christ.

Eve desired knowledge. That led her to disobey God by eating fruit from "the tree of the knowledge of good and evil." That knowledge led her away from close fellowship with God, and it didn't help her respond to life's circumstances God's way. Only godly wisdom does that.

You can be considered very knowledgeable and labeled an expert just by knowing more than most people about a subject. Scientific research is all about the search for knowledge. But without wisdom, you're just crammed with facts. Wisdom interprets that knowledge so you know what to do with it and so you know how it pertains to God.

You can gather knowledge through studying books, listening to lectures, and observing and analyzing the way the world works. Discipline of your body, mind, and spirit helps you gain knowledge. You gain the best knowledge through meditating on God's Word and by asking for the illumination of the Holy Spirit; some knowledge comes straight from God to you. Reverence for God prepares the heart and mind to receive from him knowledge that leads to wisdom.

The body of knowledge available is so vast, you can never comprehend it all. It's possible to be in a lifelong, continual state of learning. When you hunger for knowledge of God and his will for you, study the life of Jesus—no knowledge available on this

> Knowledge is of two kinds: we know a subject ourselves, or we know where we can find information on it.
> **SAMUEL JOHNSON**

holiness grace mercy love faith goodness truth freedom hope
forgiveness peace humble holiness obey repent perfect submit
serve fellowship comforter transformed noble character church

His Rich Resources

> Before a word is on my tongue you know it completely, O LORD. You hem me in—behind and before; you have laid your hand upon me.
>
> Psalm 139:4–5 NIV

earth is sweeter or more profitable than knowledge of Jesus Christ. Knowledge is one virtue in a whole chain of virtues that aid in being useful in God's kingdom.

The motive for wanting more spiritual knowledge should be so you can please God by making right choices. Spiritual knowledge leads to wisdom and godliness as well. Knowledge is what's stored in the mind. When knowledge is applied to action, wisdom is needed. Wisdom is knowing a godly goal and reaching it by a godly method. Wisdom is the knowledge of what to do next. As you seek knowledge, ask for wisdom too.

🔒

All knowledge comes from God, whether facts about the world or spiritual insight given by the Holy Spirit. Knowledge of God is the beginning of wisdom. Some knowledge gives you choices—for instance, the knowledge of good versus evil. You can learn what things to love and to hate. You can know what activities are healthy and harmful. You can determine what issues you should care about and which ones to ignore.

words
to live by

Things you might not know about *knowledge:*

❶ Computer systems are becoming smarter. Companies are creating programs that either think for themselves or try to guess what the user wants. In some cases, a computer uses "fuzzy logic" to make decisions. These are precursors to what some call artificial intelligence (AI).

❷ It is a myth that the brain deteriorates after a certain age and begins to lose its functions, including memory and knowledge. You may lose nerves, but the brain finds new pathways to function. If you exercise the brain, you increase the number of connections.

From century to century this has become more manifest; knowledge without wisdom produces external and internal self-destruction.
PAUL TILLICH

Understanding is knowing what to do. Wisdom is knowing what to do next. Virtue is actually doing it.
TRISTAN GULBERD

The wise accumulate knowledge—a true treasure; know-it-alls talk too much—a sheer waste.
Proverbs 10:14
THE MESSAGE

God, help me to make my way in this day and to respond by your wisdom in all that I face. Most of all, I desire knowledge of you and how to please you.
Amen.

knowl·edge

Many More Choices

lib·er·ty, noun.

1. permission to do a certain thing.
2. the privilege of individual rights.
3. the right of speaking without restraint.
4. *Biblical:* the power to do anything within the bounds of God's Word.
5. *Personal:* the opportunity to make good choices that open up God's possibilities.

l i b · e r · t y

There is now no condemnation for those who are in Christ Jesus, because through Christ Jesus the law of the Spirit of life set me free from the law of sin and death.
Romans 8:1–2 NIV

words
to live by

Liberty is often taken for granted by citizens in "the land of the free," but liberty is a treasured gift in countries ruled by oppressive dictators. And it seems like an impossible dream for those who find themselves confined, imprisoned, or trapped. Liberty is a precious gift for the Christian. The salvation of Jesus offers great liberty to make right choices.

The liberty the Bible talks about gives the believer freedom from the rigid interpretations of the Old Testament law. No longer must you meet rigorous demands to gain God's favor. You have the liberty and power to be delivered from sin and the clutches of the evil one, and you no longer need to be in bondage to corrupt practices. Your liberty saves you from legalism, which is the religion of rules, of do's and don'ts.

You've got liberty to be part of a great spiritual adventure, to get involved with what God is doing in your world. Some people use their liberty as a license to do anything they want, anytime they want, which leads to rebellion against any restriction or control. But license is a trapdoor—and on the other side is quicksand. Someone in the crowd taunts you, "Come with us and live like you used to. Your God will forgive you—no big deal." You're free to tell them no and mean it. Why use your liberty in that way? It does no spiritual good for anyone. There're no great rewards, except a burned-out evening or life. You're free to make other choices and to find other friends who'll encourage you in activities that won't cause you shame or ensnare you. You can use your liberty to accomplish great things, not spend it all on the narrow strictures of your own appetite.

Liberty comes from God's Word—its principles eliminate lots of bad choices. Liberty comes from Jesus, who sets captives of all kinds free. Wherever the Spirit of the Lord is, there is liberty—you're free to follow where the Spirit leads you.

How do you get to the place that you live to the full extent of your spiritual liberty? Just as a citizen of a free country, you stay within certain guiding rules and get as involved as you can. A citizen who wants to keep her liberty goes to the polls, attends the church of her choice, pays her taxes, honors her leaders, supports the fighting troops, and speaks up when she has something to

> You should always consider the honor of God, which honor grow the greater if [you are seen] for the sake of the honor of God not using your liberty.
> HULDRYCH ZWINGLI

ess grace mercy love faith goodness truth freedom hope
orgiveness peace humble holiness obey repent perfect submit
serve fellowship comforter transformed noble character church

Many More Choices

say. Live out your freedom in Christ as fully as you can—to develop and use your talents, to reach out with acts of love, to be an active encourager, even to risk your life because you've been liberated from the fear of death.

Liberty was given to you so you can be independent of the lures of the world, unrestricted in following the Holy Spirit, and uncontrolled by Satan and all his oppression. You have liberty to make choices that are good for you. You have full liberty to "go, and sin no more." This liberty opens your life to every possibility because God's in it.

> In him [Jesus] and through faith in him we may approach God with freedom and confidence.
> **Ephesians 3:12** NIV

You are liberated from your self-centeredness, your heart is free to do loving acts, and your mind is free to make good choices. You can walk on the road of God's adventure for you. You can develop your abilities for the benefit of others. And you have the freedom to go wherever the Holy Spirit leads you.

words
to live by

Things you might not know about *liberty:*

❶ One of the triumphs of the American Revolution was the passage of the Virginia Statute for Religious Liberty in 1786, which Thomas Jefferson, the original author, proudly printed in the French *Encyclopedie*. It meant people were free to follow the dictates of their own religious consciences.

❶ A maxim that is considered the common law of the land and found in the Bouvier Law Dictionary, *libertas inaestimabilis res est*, translates "liberty is a thing of inestimable value" or "liberty is a thing beyond all price."

The theological idea of freedom comes to mean deliverance from all created forces that would prevent [us] from serving and enjoying [our] Creator.
J. I. PACKER

The good news of the gospel is all about God making people whole and setting them free from prisons of sin, self, fear, and death.
GEORGE CAREY

Use your freedom to serve one another in love; that's how freedom grows.
Galatians 5:13
THE MESSAGE

God, I love you. I praise you for the freedom to walk with you and find your perfect will for my life. I choose you again today.
Amen.

lib·er·ty

A Close and Voluntary Bond

loy·al·ty, noun.

1. a close and voluntary relationship.
2. feelings of devotion, attachment, affection.
3. the keeping of one's word or vows.
4. *Biblical:* paying homage to God alone as your King and Lord.
5. *Personal:* standing by a person, cause, or fellowship.

loy·al·ty

Let love and faithfulness never leave you; bind them around your neck, write them on the tablet of your heart.
Proverbs 3:3 NIV

words
to live by

They stand before the judge, these ones who've come from countries all over the world. They raise their right hands and recite the oath of allegiance. They are now new citizens of the United States. They must obey its laws, pay its taxes, and support its government. They offer their faithfulness and devotion. They have chosen loyalty to another nation, a different flag.

The Hebrew word *hesed* is often translated "loyalty," but it isn't equivalent to any English concept. Other options include an act of "duty" or "mercy." *Hesed* always has to do with relationships and is an action, not an attitude or verbal promise. Loyalty is the faithfulness of people who fulfill their obligations, even when it's difficult. In Scriptures, loyalty is "a firm place" into which an unmovable, firmly anchored peg will be driven, even though it's pushed so hard that it breaks off at the point of entry. Loyalty is a dependable servant, a faithful Christian witness, or a trusted and wise manager. Jesus asks for loyalty with his cry "Follow me!"

Loyalty is someone who stands by you, no matter what. The apostle Paul pleaded for help from another loyal worker to mediate between two women, Euodia and Syntyche, who fought with each other but had both been loyal to Paul by contending at his side for the Gospel's sake. He didn't turn against them because of their flaws.

Loyalty calls for sacrifice that is often generated by a request. Jonathan asked his good friend David to deal loyally with members of his family by providing for their needs if he died, which David did.

Loyalty is believing in someone enough to help her become who God created her to be. Loyalty is lending strength, respect, and support that provides confidence to compete, strive, and risk. Loyalty is devoted love, especially in times of failure or embarrassment. Love is the basic language and loyalty the critical bedrock of relationships.

Partisanship can seem like loyalty, but it's more a dogmatic prejudice than a heart-felt, sincere commitment. People aren't as important as the project. The project's just a bolster of pride and stubborn bias. Loyalty is uniting in a common goal because of shared faith, a belief in ministry, and the call of God.

> Every legitimate loyalty . . . has its source and completion in the loyalty due to the living God and Father of all men.
> S. PARKES CADMAN

123

ess grace mercy love faith goodness truth freedom hope
orgiveness peace humble holiness obey repent perfect submit
serve fellowship comforter transformed noble character church

A Close and Voluntary Bond

Love the LORD, all
you who belong to
him. The LORD
protects those who
truly believe.
Psalm 31:23 NCV

Loyalty can be cultivated. First, you make a long-term commitment to someone or something other than yourself, by the leading of God. Then when a test comes, you prove that loyalty by staying true. If you're loyal, you can be trusted, believed, relied upon. You have established yourself as a person who is dependable. You keep your promise. You support your friend. You're a faithful spouse. However, it's not wise to depend on your own ability to stay loyal. Put your trust in God's power to work through that relationship or stick with that cause. If God appointed it for his purpose, you'll gain the strength from him to stay firm when you're sorely tried—and great is your faithfulness.

To be loyal is to be dependable, faithful, and trustworthy. Loyalty is sincere allegiance and heartfelt devotion to a person or cause. Loyalty begins with a long-term commitment that you believe is God's will. Loyalty is developed by promise-keeping and standing true when tests come. Loyalty is persistent love in the face of faults.

words
to live by

Things you might not know about *loyalty:*

❶ May 1 of each year has been proclaimed by Congress and the President as Loyalty Day. Americans reaffirm their allegiance to their country and resolve to uphold the vision of their forefathers.

❶ The Loyalty Islands are east of mainland New Caledonia. The islands were so named when discovered in late eighteenth century by British merchant ships that found the people of dual Melanesian and Polynesian heritage to be "honest and dependable." They're known for legendary friendliness to visitors.

The greater the loyalty of a group toward the group . . . the greater the probability that the group will achieve its goals.
RENSIS LIKERT

Loyalty has three faces: devotion to a person, allegiance to a kingdom or cause, and faithfulness to one's obligations.
DONALD E. HOKE

I'm so grateful to Christ Jesus for making me adequate to do this work. He went out on a limb, you know, in trusting me with this ministry.
1 Timothy 1:12
THE MESSAGE

God, I want to be a loyal friend. I want to be faithful in all the relationships that you have brought into my life. Most of all, I want to be true to you in my heart, my words, and my deeds.
Amen.

l o y · a l · t y

---

mer·cy, noun.

1. a disposition to be kind and forgiving.
2. the relief of suffering.
3. a lenient sentence for a criminal.
4. **Biblical:** compassion and pardon by God.
5. **Personal:** obeying God's call to benefit someone in trouble.

m e r · c y

The LORD God has told us what is right and what he demands: "See that justice is done, let mercy be your first concern, and humbly obey your God." Micah 6:8 CEV

She's young, pregnant, unmarried. Her family kicked her out because they warned her about that guy, forbade her to go out with him. She's scared and angry. But she's on your doorstep because her boyfriend dumped her too. You wonder if you'd be seen as condoning her action by taking her in. Yet you don't waver to show her mercy, because she's so pitiful, and for the sake of the baby. But what about the boyfriend? And the family? Will you show them mercy, too, if they ask for it?

Mercy's not easy to give when you know what's been done.

God's mercy shines in the Old Testament. His just anger is always tempered with mercy, which he delights to give. Mercy is God's love and kindness, his faithfulness and goodness shown to people who've done grave wrong. The word *mercy* is often translated as "grace" in the New Testament. Mercy is generosity to a weaker party who seeks a protector.

words
to live by

Mercy implies action beyond the rule of law. God offers mercy to anyone who sincerely asks for it—to be redeemed from sins, to be saved from enemies, to find relief in troubles. Mercy is one of God's most persistent acts, and it is his mercy that brings you salvation.

It's possible to show mercy even while abhorring a person's sins and its consequences. Zechariah prophesied that the Messiah would come to deliver people from sin and Satan's oppression because of God's tender mercy. Throughout Jesus' ministry on earth, people cried out to him for mercy and received it.

You should show mercy like Jesus does. However, mercy-giving can pit you against people and get you into controversy. Others may have a different take on the recipient's situation. They may resent that the full and proper sentence wasn't served. They may consider you naïve and not aware of all the facts. Their prejudice, anger, or bitterness may blind them to your sincere motives.

Mercy is not a feeling; it doesn't occur unless there's an action. You determine to show mercy, despite the facts of the case, because God leads you. Confession and repentance, which presuppose guilt, come before mercy. And there's a legal system in the land that's put in place to accomplish God's purposes too. Justice works, when the punishment fits the crime. But if you have any say in the matter, or any power at

> Being the children of their Father in heaven, [the merciful will] go on to show mercy, even to their enemies. They must give like God, and like God be blessed in giving.
> **George MacDonald**

The Power of Compassion

all in the outcome, try to err on the side of mercy.

Some steps can help in doing mercy. Prepare your mind for the action you are about to take by asking God to see the person and all the circumstances from his point of view. Release the offender, in the name of Jesus, to God's care. Pray that the Holy Spirit will go ahead of you to prepare the heart of the one who will receive the mercy act, so that the most possible spiritual good can result. Ask the Lord for wisdom in how to reply when detractors ask, "Why did you do this?" Pray that God will receive honor.

Be merciful, just as your father is merciful.
Luke 6:36 NIV

❶

Mercy is compassion to those entrapped in some difficulty, even if it's their own fault. Abounding in mercy is one of God's central characteristics. You should show mercy like Jesus did. Mercy expresses God's goodness toward the guilty and miserable, not just because of their wretched condition, but because of his love. Mercy is the outward show of pity by someone with the power to bestow it in practical ways.

words
to live by

Things you might not know about *mercy:*

❶ The Latin word for *mercy* is *misericordia,* and there are many shelters, hospitals, and care homes with this name, such as Misericordia/Heart of Mercy in Chicago, which supports individuals with developmental disabilities to maximize their level of independence by promoting natural family and community involvement.

❶ The ancient Roman society spoke of four cardinal virtues: wisdom, justice, temperance, and courage—but not mercy. The Romans despised pity. The Greeks held similar views. They thought mercy indicated weakness rather than strength. Aristotle wrote that pity was a troublesome emotion.

m e r . c y

Mercy's gate opens to those who knock.
C. H. SPURGEON

Mercy among the virtues is like the moon among the stars, not so sparkling and vivid as many, but dispensing a calm radiance that hallows the whole.
EDWIN HUBBELL CHAPIN

God loved us so much that he made us alive with Christ, and God's wonderful kindness is what saves you.
Ephesians 2:5 CEV

God, give me the courage to show mercy to those caught in traps of their own making. Help me remember your times of mercy shown to me so that I can go and do likewise.
Amen.

A Gift With a Purpose

mon·ey, noun.

1. anything that serves as a common medium of exchange.
2. purchasing power.
3. a system of coinage.
4. *Biblical:* a temporary, limited resource for living.
5. *Personal:* one of God's gifts.

mon·ey

You cannot be the slave of two masters. You will like one more than the other or be more loyal to one than the other. You cannot serve both God and money.
Matthew 16:13 CEV

If you're like most people, you feel uncomfortable talking about money, especially yours. You may think about it, whether you've got a lot of it or not, because money influences how you live. It provides your sense of worth, in some ways. A salary defines how valued you are in the workplace, if you compare it with that of your co-workers. But most of all, your attitude toward money corresponds with the intensity and direction of your spiritual walk.

It's hard to make spiritual sense about money, unless you assess its value from God's point of view. The possession of money and goods was frequently looked upon in the Bible as an indication of God's blessing. The idea expressed by wealth sometimes indicates a feeling of well-being, but usually it means the traditional "to possess riches." The Bible emphasizes that money should never dominate a believer's life because of its limited,

words
to live by

temporary nature. Your attitude toward money provides a major test of your true heart's desires (1 Timothy 6:17 NIV). Jesus condemned the man who spent all his money building bigger barns and neglected being rich toward God.

A good example of the use of money is Barnabas's selling a field and donating the proceeds to encourage the fellowship and further God's kingdom. A bad example is Ananias and Sapphira doing the exact same thing, except for their motive of self-glory.

Many warnings in God's Word are directed at the rich because of what loving money does to the heart. And yet money and wealth are considered by most people to open the door wide to happiness, security, and contentment. Someone wisely countered, "The real measure of your wealth is how much you'd be worth if you lost all your money."

How you manage your money reaps financial benefits. Gratitude for what you have, acknowledging it all comes from God, reaps spiritual rewards, and how you use your money tests your trustworthiness. The purpose of money is for survival and comfort and to further God's kingdom. Loving money too much messes you up spiritually and distorts your vision of who you are. Money attachment can neutralize the power of God's Word in your life.

The best attitude toward money is to place all your holdings in God's hands and

> Every time you spend money, you're casting a vote for the kind of world you want.
> ANNA LAPPE

A Gift With a Purpose

to release every cent to him to use as he directs. Give some of it away, but with a willing spirit. God loves a cheerful giver.

Acquire wisdom in managing your money with classes, books, advisers. However, don't be consumed with this part of it either. Glorify God with your money. Acknowledge his generosity in providing it for you. The gift of money is a test. It reveals your stewardship ability and the priorities of your heart. When you love money too much, it becomes an idol. It replaces God as the center of your affections. You depend on it to take care of you instead.

> Tell [those rich in this world's wealth] to go after God, who piles on all the riches we could ever manage.
> **I Timothy 6:17**
> THE MESSAGE

O

Money is a possession that tests your heart. Learn the financial and spiritual value of money by assessing it from God's point of view. The Bible says you have the right to do with your money whatever you determine you can do cheerfully. To develop the best attitude, acknowledge your money all comes from God, give it back to him, then dispense it at his direction; that will give God the glory.

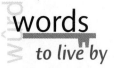

words
to live by

etcetera . . .

Things you might not know about *money:*

● Mary Hunt, who once struggled with acquiring a monumental debt with out-of-control expenditures, now counsels women on how to gain financial freedom. Her book *The Financially Confident Woman* spells out nine principles to find hope in managing money.

● A new breed of financial experts who call themselves "wealth counselors" advise that being flooded with a sudden fortune, whether earned or inherited, can be highly stressful. Like any drug, money can distort your life—especially in large quantities. A windfall "changes all the parameters of how you live."

I believe that the power to make money is a gift from God.
JOHN D. ROCKEFELLER

While wealth is a gift of God, it is never a blessing if we keep it to ourselves.
KENNETH S. KANTZER

God loves the person who gives cheerfully. And God will generously provide all you need.
2 Corinthians 9:7 NLT

God, I thank you so much for all you've given me. I give it back to you. Guide me in the uses of my money and possessions. Amen.

m o n · e y

Moods That Surround Your Moves

mo·tives, noun.
_____

1. the reasons for your action.
2. impulses; desires.
3. predominate intentions.
4. **Biblical:** the hidden purposes of the human heart.
5. **Personal:** the true stimuli behind your deeds and words.

mo·tives

Acknowledge the God of your father, and serve him with wholehearted devotion and with a willing mind, for the LORD searches every heart and understands every motive behind the thoughts.
1 Chronicles 28:9 NIV

Suppose you're a speaker and you expected a huge crowd, but only a dozen showed up because of poor advertising. You're disheartened. This had been your big opportunity to address an important subject before lots of folks. You toy with the idea of shortening the talk and scooting out early. Why give your all for so few? But then you notice an elderly woman with a cane struggle up to the front of the room. She sits down with a smile beamed on you, pulls out a notebook, and begins to write. Your adrenaline flows. You decide to give your full spiel after all. You determine it's worth it even for just this one.

Motives are the hidden incentives inside the secret places of the heart that push, pull, and manipulate what you say or do. The Hebrew word *yetser* comes closest to the English word *motives*. It means "a form that frames a purpose," "an intellectual framework." Motives are pur-

words
to live by

poses formed out of the imagination and desires of the heart. Motives are the frame for your words and actions. They surround everything that you are.

Motives arise from within you but are often incited by some outside influence. Jesus rebuked Peter when he discerned behind Peter's words of admonition that his motives were influenced by Satan. Your motives are constantly affected by the persuasions of the people and the messages that fill your daily environment.

Motives are your main concerns, the purposes behind your words and actions. They are the ambitions that drive your decisions. Motives reveal your priorities and indicate who is most important. When you line your motives up with God's, you know you are in his perfect will and giving him first place.

It is hard to take when someone accuses you of a certain motive and you believe it's not true. They may think you were trying to deceive them when perhaps you were just careless or acted from the wrong information. Your motives may be elusive, sometimes even to yourself. It takes sorting out your thoughts and quieting yourself before the Lord to assess what they are. Motives need to be surrendered to him so he can purify them. Probing by God's Spirit or through those close to you may draw them out.

Work to change the attitude of your thoughts. Determine how much you're affected by the behavior, habits, and

The tragic truth is that often those we serve can detect more quickly than anyone else whether or not our actions are done in love or not.
W. PHILLIP KELLER

ness grace mercy love faith goodness truth freedom hope
orgiveness peace humble holiness obey repent perfect submit
serve fellowship comforter transformed noble character church

customs of people around you in your responses to life, and ask God to help you sort out your thought patterns—what is pleasing to him and what is not. Always include God in every decision and aim to do what he wants first and foremost. You can change your motives. Stop and listen to your heart. Pay attention to what the Holy Spirit reveals. Then give yourself with enthusiasm to the task at hand, under the strength of the right motive.

God not only knows, but he understand your motives, even when you don't, even if you try to hide them. God is stronger than your motives; his purposes will prevail.

Mixed motives twist life into tangles; pure motives take you straight down the road.
Proverbs 21:8
THE MESSAGE

Motives are the reasons why you do and say certain things. On the surface, your actions may be interpreted one way, but the purpose behind them may be quite different. God, through those close to you, can draw out your motives. Often your motives are developed through influences around you. When you allow the Holy Spirit to control your mind, he purifies your motives.

words
to live by

Things you might not know about *motives:*

❶ The Reiss Profile interpretation and scoring software was developed to reveal the most important motives and values that guide a person's behavior. It tells you who a person is. Based on one hundred items completed by raters, it is used to assess roommate compatibility, challenging behavior patterns, and what makes you happy.

❶ Polls consistently place privacy among Internet users' foremost concerns. Users fear that Web sites abuse their power to collect and distribute personal information, putting profit motives above privacy interests. According to the FTC, self-regulation has failed.

We should often be ashamed of our finest actions if the world understood our motives.
FRANÇOIS DE LA ROCHEFOUCAULD

Never ascribe to an opponent motives meaner than your own.
JOHN M. BARRIE

Someone's thoughts may be as deep as the ocean, but if you are smart, you will discover them.
Proverbs 20:5 CEV

God, search my heart to see if what I'm doing is for the right reasons. Purify my motives. Cleanse my purposes.
Amen.

m o · t i v e s

Of Greatness and Grandeur
(words)

no·ble, adjective.

1. lofty, exalted character.
2. showing magnanimity.
3. generous and ethical.
4. **Biblical:** the description of a believer who's cleansed for God's use.
5. **Personal:** a greatness of soul developed through spiritual obedience.

n o · b l e

Whatever is true, whatever is noble, whatever is right, whatever is pure, whatever is lovely, whatever is admirable—if anything is excellent or praiseworthy—think about such things.
Philippians 4:8 NIV

Think of your planet as it is, in all its gore and glory, and ponder what would make it a better place. In some minds, it would have no wars. The earth's occupants would enjoy peace and calm all the time. In that reality, the leaders of the nations would need to be honorable people. Such words as *corruption* and *greed* would not exist in anyone's vocabulary. Love and integrity would govern every law, every intent of the heart. In other words, the world would be populated and ruled by only noble people.

Three Hebrew words express the meaning of *noble: addir, yaqar,* and *chayil.* They describe a stately one, precious and rare, with strength, ability, and efficiency like the force of an army. *Noble* is applied to the Messiah, who is "glorious." The name of Jesus is noble and should be highly honored. The Greek words *eugenes* and *kratistos* distinguish noble as "of a well-

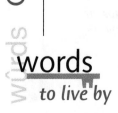

words
to live by

born family" or "most excellent." However, the Bible discourages appointing special privileges to believers who are rich or of high class. In fact, anyone can be noble. God delights in choosing and using humbler servants.

To be noble is to act with lofty motives for a worthy cause. To be noble is to be devoted, faithful, honest, and brave.

Haman relished his position. He rubbed shoulders with the nobility of his day. When he boasted before King Xerxes of the honors to be given to the "noble princes," he meant himself. But the king chose Mordecai, the Jew. In no way noble by birth, Mordecai was noble by virtue.

The common notion of *noble* indicates outward appearances only—anything that looks "regal," including fanfare, formality, titles, or attire. To be noble often infers haughtiness because of station in society or demeanor. In Europe, where one can be born into or appointed to nobility, an interesting phrase is used: *noblesse oblige*, which asserts that benevolent and honorable behavior is considered the responsibility of persons of high birth or rank. That is, nobility should behave nobly toward others to offset the tendency to think of themselves as not needing anyone, including the Lord.

How does an ordinary woman become noble? She cleanses herself from sin through discipline and dependence on God's Spirit, to be used for his noble purposes. A noble woman chooses the high

An absolute need exists for noble Christian women with strong judgment and large scientific attainment to occupy the professional field as earnest co-laborers with their brothers.
SARAH A. COLBY

ness grace mercy love faith goodness truth freedom hope
orgiveness peace humble holiness obey repent perfect submit
serve fellowship comforter transformed noble character church

Of Greatness and Grandeur

ground of honor, by showing respect to everyone in her world. She becomes an example to other believers through her open, honest responses to God's Word. The noble-minded are eager for spiritual teaching and test it against God's Word.

The noble woman admires other noble women and follows their example. The noble woman survives with dignity the cruelties of her world, her soul protected because she insists on seeing beauty when others feel only dread. The noble woman exhibits a calm, steady character. She sits quietly before God and pays attention to what he tells her. She finds comfort from him in lonely, hurting experiences. She lets go of the concerns that threaten to dim trust in him.

> The seeds that were planted on good ground are people who also hear the word. But they keep it in their good and honest hearts and produce what is good despite what life may bring.
> Luke 8:15
> GOD'S WORD

To be noble has nothing to do with wealth, position, or title. To be noble involves inner strength, might of character, and the ability to stay steady in life's storms. These qualities are developed by the application of spiritual disciplines. The woman who wants to be noble confesses and repents of known sin, studies role models for clues, and sits at the feet of Jesus.

words
to live by

etcetera . . .

Things you might not know about *noble:*

❶ Queen Elizabeth I was stingy about granting peerages and rarely granted land gifts to accompany such honors, so there were fewer noblemen and noblewomen in her day. When Sir Henry Sidney was offered a barony without property, his wife dissuaded the queen; they couldn't afford to maintain the higher title.

❷ These are the five titles for noblewomen, or peeresses, of the British Nobility, with the dates they were first created and in order of importance: Duchess (1337), Marchioness (1385), Countess (circa 1000), Viscountess (1440), and Lady (1066).

[The gift of making friends involves,] above all, the power of going out of one's self, and appreciating whatever is noble and loving in another.
THOMAS HUGHES

Would'st thou clearly learn what true nobility is? Inquire of noble-minded women.
GERMAN SAYING

A wife of noble character who can find? She is worth far more than rubies. Her husband has full confidence in her and lacks nothing of value.
Proverbs 31:10–11 NIV

God, I bow before you now without any pretenses. I thank you for noble women around me and down through the church age who encourage me to nobler living. Let me be like them.
Amen.

n o · b l e

Surrender Thoughtfully

o·bey, *verb.*

1. to carry out an order.
2. to follow after.
3. to yield, to submit.
4. *Biblical:* to hear, to believe, to act upon the words of God.
5. *Personal:* to be persuaded to act in trust that God knows what's best for you.

o · bey

[Jesus] learned obedience from what he suffered and, once made perfect, he became the source of eternal salvation for all who obey him.
Hebrews 5:8–9 NIV

Human nature bristles at obedience from the first moment a baby's told, "Don't touch!" From then on, obedience seems like such a drag: "Look before you cross the street." "You can't play the song if you don't learn the notes." "Follow the doctor's orders."

Understanding the reasons why one should obey improves the willing obedience ratio. Other times, a little persuasion goes a long way.

The Hebrew *shama* means "to hear," "to listen to," "to obey." Obedience comes in stages. First, to hear is "to gain knowledge" from the Lord. Then, to listen to is "to pay close attention," "to hearken," or "to agree with the intentions of the petition." Obedience requires active listening. In the case of hearing and listening to a higher authority, *shama* leads to "obey." For example, God promised that all nations would be blessed because

words
to live by

Abraham heard, listened to, and obeyed God's voice.

The Greek word *peitho* contains another aspect of obedience: "to be persuaded." Understanding that leads to agreement is needed to cooperate enough to obey, especially when there's reticence to trust the one giving the order.

The steps to obedience happened in one moment for Mary. When the angel told her she would have a child, she asked one question: "How will this be since I am a virgin?" She needed understanding to be persuaded. When the angel explained the spiritual dimension, Mary submitted. She heard, she listened, she was persuaded: she obeyed instantly.

Some folks around you may never attempt to obey God. They react by doing what seems right to them. Three different voices try to persuade you to follow. Your own whiney speech may be full of "me, me, me" talk. Satan's taunts are usually seductive, insistent, and insistent that you decide in a hurry. God's voice rings loving and clear but firm and agrees with his Word. But obeying God is a challenge. It often accompanies sacrifice—something is given up, one path is chosen over another, you lose something before you realize your gain. Depending on your trust factor, you may need convincing. Fill yourself with God's Word on the subject—obedient believers are thinking people. But a word of caution: delayed obedience becomes disobedience.

Obedience begins in the mind and the

What our nation needs most right now is a movement of people motivated not by short-term success, but by obedience, demonstrating a holy perseverance that only God himself can give.
CHARLES COLSON

143

Surrender Thoughtfully

My child, remember my teachings and instructions and obey them completely. They will help you live a long and prosperous life.
Proverbs 3:1–2 CEV

thoughts, but soon it can be seen. When you obey, you prove your faith in God. As you practice biblical obedience in small steps, you learn to trust God more quickly and recognize his utterances out of the crowd. You also realize his instructions aren't power controls; they're born out of his love to bring you life, not grief.

Obedience has its own rewards. When you obey God he promises all kinds of blessings. You'll know God's peace and joy. You'll feel his smile. You'll watch as you avoid all those disasters and sorrows that disobedience brings. Obedience to God is a pleasure beyond comparison to any other joy on earth. Obedience is easy when you love God, when your faith is wholly placed in him.

Obedience is stepping out in trust to follow God's commands. It is believing God knows what's best for you. First, you hear his voice; second, you listen. If you're having a difficult time with a particular issue of obedience, you may need persuasion. It's so much easier to obey when you're convinced God's way is smart, productive, and fulfills a greater purpose. But to delay may entice you to disobey. You prove your love for him by obedience.

words *to live by*

etcetera . . .

Things you might not know about *obey:*

❶ Newton discovered that your body obeys the law of motion. When riding in a car at fifty m.p.h., you move at the same speed. If the driver suddenly brakes, the car stops, but your body continues forward at fifty m.p.h., unless it is restrained by a seat belt.

❶ Puppy kindergartens promise positive obedience training to break any dog of undesirable behavior such as barking, howling, digging, whining, chewing, soiling, jumping, and hyperactivity. They use behavior-modification techniques that look at the problems from the dog's point of view.

Don't look to God as the stern taskmaster who demands our obedience, but as the loving Father who wins it.
HANNAH WHITALL SMITH

The value of obedience depends on its quality. If obedience is poky, it is second rate. If it is sour, it is of no account. Obedience must be swift and glad.
CHARLES JEFFERSON

Obey your leaders and do what they say. They are watching over you, and they must answer to God.
Hebrews 13:17 CEV

God, give me understanding of your commands.
Help me when I'm confused, when I'm tempted,
when I'm torn in different directions. I submit
myself to the process of your persuasion.
Amen.

o · b e y

A Gentle Endurance

pa·tience, noun.

1. tranquil waiting or expectation.
2. composure during a long seige.
3. tolerant understanding.
4. *Biblical:* knowing God has everything under control.
5. *Personal:* waiting without complaint for God's perfect timing.

pa·tience

God has chosen you and made you his holy people. He loves you. So always do these things: Show mercy to others, be kind, humble, gentle, and patient. Get along with each other, and forgive each other.
Colossians 3:12–13
NCV

The more expensive technologies you own, the greater conveniences you possess, the fancier bells and whistles on the appliances, the more patience you need. Machines break. Computers melt down. Electrical things burn out. And socks still disappear in clothes dryers. Even the joys of microwave meals, mall shopping, and solving problems in half-hour segments on TV contribute to your lack of patience.

The Greek word for *patience* is *makrothumia*, which means "forbearance" and "long-suffering" and usually refers to God. Human long-suffering conveys the enlarged capacity to absorb temporary irritants in order to cheerfully lean forward to see what God is going to do. Patience is a kind of gentle endurance.

Saints of God are required to be patient, to not surrender to circumstances or succumb under trial, because life is tough. The saints of the Bible combine patience with hope. God is patient with weakness, failure, and sin and still pursues his plans, in spite of everything that goes wrong. Your patience should spring out of this divine example.

It's a challenge to practice patience, to keep from griping while biding your time. Patience can seem like hanging loose, a kind of apathy, even laziness. But God-centered patience has goals, plans, and dreams that watch for perfect timing. That kind of patience seeks wisdom in knowing when all the factors are right to forge ahead. You keep thinking things through until you see the path more clearly. Patience stops, waits, and listens, even when someone else might consider that being slow.

When your way's wonderful, you don't need patience. Patience needs a goal to see beyond what's happening right now. Seeing a bigger picture strengthens the resolve, encourages patient plodding.

Patience and peace are two sides of a similar virtue. Love needs patience to complete its work, and patience works well with faith in receiving God's promises. Patience has to do with time. Time flies; time drags. It's hard to wait when you feel the marching pace of time, no matter what its pace. Your age and circumstances change as the days pass. Patience is hard for clock people, those who measure and manage each minute and feel their hours brimming full of important busyness.

The patient learn to use their time for other duties and concerns while God works behind the scenes on the thing you care about most. The patient occupy their

Do not lose courage in considering your own imperfections but instantly set about remedying them—every day begin the task anew.
SAINT FRANCIS DE SALES

A Gentle Endurance

Let patience have her perfect work, that ye may be perfect and entire, wanting nothing.

James 1:4 KJV

attention until God gives further instructions. If activity is impossible, allow him to do his work in your inner self, such as correct all your negative thinking by giving your mind constructive assignments.

God has all the time he needs to accomplish his purposes for you and those you love. Meanwhile, he has reasons to make you wait. It takes time to work on stubborn wills. The complexity of the consequences of sin don't get fixed overnight. Besides, he has your own attitudes and your relationship with him to consider too. Ask him what he wants of you while you linger and lament.

❶

A holy God is patient with sinners, so you can learn patience too. Patience is more than just waiting around; it's being cheerful and productive and working on your inner life as God works out things behind the scenes for the perfecting of your goals. Time marches on and so should you, by keeping time to God's beat. Rewards are up ahead for those who patiently wait.

words
to live by

Things you might not know about *patience:*

🟠 "Idiot's delight" and "patience" are British alternative names for almost all basic solitaire card games that are played by only one player.

🟠 Thomas Edison conducted countless experiments in search of an effective filament to use in carbon incandescent lamps. As each fiber failed, he tossed it out his window. The pile of failures reached to the second story of his house before his patience won out and he found the right one.

God aims to exalt Himself by working for those who wait for Him.
JOHN PIPER

If you trust God and believe that He is working, regardless of what you see, hear or feel, you will be able to handle each day as it comes.
STEVEN S. FOSTER

Walk worthy of the calling with which you were called.
Ephesians 4:1 NKJV

God, as your servant Peter Marshall prayed, so do I pray now: teach me, O Lord, the disciplines of patience, for to wait is often harder than to work.
Amen.

p·a·t·i·e·n·c·e

ness grace mercy love faith goodness truth freedom hope
orgiveness peace humble holiness obey repent perfect submit
serve fellowship comforter transformed noble character church

The Fight for Calm

peace, noun.

1. a settled composure.
2. serenity or harmony in the midst of enmity or strife.
3. contentment with one's earthly lot.
4. **Biblical:** reconciliation with God.
5. **Personal:** a tranquility that results from coping with stressful situations.

peace

God was pleased to have all his fullness dwell in him, and through him to reconcile to himself all things . . . by making peace through his blood, shed on the cross.
Colossians 1:19–20
NIV

Once upon a time in the land of Paradise, there lived a man and woman who knew nothing but peace. No quarrels, pressures, or irritations of any kind accosted them in their perfect home. But they don't live there anymore. And neither do you. But you can begin where they did. You can walk with God in your own spiritual Eden any moment of the day.

Peace in the New Testament describes *eirene*—a demeanor and lifestyle of quietness, rest, and contentment. *Eirene* includes the ability to trust God to help you cope with daily hassles and challenges. It's an inner repose.

The world around you salutes "Peace!" as easily as "Have a good day." But at best this expresses a mere longing or wish. The promises of peace come packaged as pills or as rainbows at the bottom of a bottle. Peace as the world views it is a state of mind generated by chemical

words
to live by

aids or temporary highs or the absence of conflict, at any cost.

You practice gaining emotional control like you improve your health, one substitution at a time. For instance, turn off the blaring TV and read an inspiring book instead. You cooperate with God in your stability, like you take care of your goods. If the windshield on your car is chipped, you relieve the pressure by repairing it before it fractures. Your mental pane's the same way— sharing with a trusted friend can relieve the pressure before little hairline cracks from stress become full breaks.

At times, God will empower you with instant calm after anxious moments, such as in a crisis when you must stay sane for the sake of others. But the attitude of peace is also a fruit of the Spirit that grows in its season, a result of plodding perseverance. The confusion of life jangles your nerves and messes with your mind. Yet you need tests to prove your mettle, to learn how to face disorder unruffled. You'll develop spiritual spunk when you seek inner stillness in the center of chaos. You learn peace while life happens.

But you must spend time with him. Jesus faced plenty of enemies, yet epitomized peace. He got away from the crowds and communed alone with the Father. He knew who held all the parts of the universal puzzle. Take a moment each day to think of nothing but God. Stand in his presence.

[The Word of God] works against anxiety, depression, defensiveness, immaturity, and all the things we routinely consider indications of a lack of mental health.
FRANK MINIRTH

...ness grace mercy love faith goodness truth freedom hope
orgiveness peace humble holiness obey repent perfect submit
serve fellowship comforter transformed noble character church

The Fight for Calm

Let the peace of Christ rule in your hearts, since as members of one body you were called to peace. And be thankful.
Colossians 3:15 NIV

Focus on who he is. Seek to know him—the depths of his interests, the span of his purposes. Picture what peace looks like to you. You may imagine some scene or recall a state of mind. Or you may remember some person. What memories or characteristics trigger your thoughts?

True peace resounds out of a teachable spirit, when you quiet all the clashing voices, when you persevere in prayer, when you scour the Scriptures. You get peace when you lounge in God's presence and give him a chance to hug you and say, "You are my cherished child, my treasured daughter. You're going to make it through this."

God is your peace. If you interact with him during stresses and trials, you'll discover peace as an inner coping mechanism. Peace is a mental attitude and an emotional balancer. It is also a gift from God for those who trust in Jesus Christ to save them from their sins.

words
to live by

Things you might not know about *peace:*

1 After WWII the Allied armies corralled hungry, homeless children into large camps. But the children didn't sleep well. A psychologist suggested: Let the kids hold a slice of bread every night, so they know they'll eat in the morning. The bread provided security for peaceful rest.

1 The Hebrew word *shalom* is a greeting that includes a blessing that you "be made perfect." It's a benediction for complete wholeness, that everything works together in your life as God purposed and designed it.

Never be in a hurry; do everything quietly and in a calm spirit. Do not lose your inner peace for anything whatsoever, even if your whole world seems upset.
SAINT FRANCIS DE SALES

We should establish ourselves in a sense of God's presence by continually conversing with him.
BROTHER LAWRENCE

Before you know it, a sense of God's wholeness, everything coming together for good, will come and settle you down.
Philippians 4:7
THE MESSAGE

God, you are my peace. Help me today to release each problem, every duty, the crunch of so much to do and so little time to your capable care. Keep me focused on you. Amen.

peace

The Will to Keep Running

per·sist·ence, noun.

1. the act of refusing to give up or let go.
2. the act of outlasting all the competition.
3. the act of sitting down to a task until it's done.
4. *Biblical:* the quality needed to prove your faith.
5. *Personal:* steadfast determination to resist distractions in order to reach your goal.

per·sist·ence

Jackie Joyner-Kersee, one of the world's finest athletes, has asthma. She can't take the prescription drugs to control her asthmatic attacks brought on by physical exercise because they contain substances forbidden by the Olympic Committee. In spite of this, she is a four-time Olympic champion, winning the heptathlon silver in 1984, the gold in heptathlon and long jump in 1988, and the gold again in 1992. Jackie's persistence overcame this obstacle to her goal of being a runner.

The Greek word *hupomone* in God's Word encourages the believer to persistent endurance, steadfastness, constancy, diligence, and perseverance. *Hupomone* persistence is the characteristic of a person who is not swerved from a deliberate purpose or loyalty to faith and piety by even the greatest trials and sufferings. A threefold dimension to this kind of persistence includes perseverance (patient endurance

To those who by persistence in doing good seek glory, honor and immortality, he will give eternal life.
Romans 2:7 NLT

words
to live by

in the face of opposition, obstacles, or objections), steadfastness (firmly fixed in faith or devotion to duty), and diligence (long, steady application of effort to a godly purpose).

In the book of Ezra, encouraged by the exhortation of the prophets Zechariah and Haggai, the Jewish exiles persisted to restore the rundown Jerusalem temple, in spite of much fierce opposition, such as a constant fire of harassment. Ezra, the overseer of the project, wrote of this in a letter to King Darius: "this work goes on with diligence."

The long run of faith is a tough, uphill stretch. Persistence is essential for the Christian disciple in order to become mature, complete in Christ. The power of any ministry evolves through persistence. If heaven is your destination and holiness is your path, then persistence is the transportation that gets you there. You'll need to push with persistence to stay on spiritual track to the very end. Along the way, you need persistence in controlling your thoughts, your words, and your actions and in purifying your motives.

There's a difference between perseverance and obstinacy—one comes from a strong will, the other from a strong won't. Obstinacy is born of pride or prejudice and keeps at a position or project in spite of considerations that should induce one to desist. Obstinacy is inflexible, adamant, rigid. Persistence is sticking with a good, godly goal that gets tougher to reach than first

If I had to select one quality, one personal characteristic that I regard as being most highly correlated with success, whatever the field, I would pick the trait of persistence.
RICHARD M. DEVOS

mercy love faith goodness truth freedom hope
orgiveness peace humble holiness obey repent perfect submit
serve fellowship comforter transformed noble character church

The Will to Keep Running

> Let us not be weary in well doing: for in due season we shall reap, if we faint not.
>
> **Galatians 6:9** KJV

expected. Persistence is trying again when you fail, after assessing what went wrong. Persistence is doing your best, where you are, with what you have. You gain toughening up of your spirit when you take breaks for prayer and meditation of God's Word and for self-examination and confession. Spiritual persistence comes down to the choice to press onward one day at a time.

Persistence needs a high motivation, a purpose that you really want to fulfill. You sort through a plan of how to get there, believe in it enough to explain and overcome all objections. Godly persistence prays for a steadfast spirit to manage the tyranny of your own moods and discouragements as well as outside influences. Persistence helps you turn a corner when you ascertain that you are who you are and must get on with the serious business of doing God's will.

❶

Persistence is necessary to doing any important task for God. Persistence means to remain under the responsibility, to bear up under the pressures, to stay strong, firm, and, most of all, steadfast until completion. Persistence is needed in any huge undertaking, especially if there is opposition. If you know God has ordained a certain task for you, persist to the end.

words
to live by

etcetera . . .

Things you might not know about *persistence:*

❶ Persistence of vision is the retention of an image on your eye's retina that makes it possible for pictures to "move." A motion picture is a set of still photographs shown rapidly in a series. One image overlaps another, giving the appearance of movement.

❶ Emporer Meng T'ien of China began construction of the Great Wall in 221 B.C. The last major work on the wall was completed during the Ming Dynasty around A.D. 1500. Considered one of humankind's greatest accomplishments of persistence, the Great Wall extends 1,500 miles.

Press on: nothing in the world can take the place of perseverance. Talent will not. Genius will not. Education will not. Persistence and determination alone are omnipotent.
CALVIN COOLIDGE

Persistence is the twin sister of excellence. One is a matter of quality; the other, a matter of time.
MARABEL MORGAN

You need to persevere so that when you have done the will of God, you will receive what he has promised.
Hebrews 10:36 NIV

God, fill me with your Spirit's strength today so I can have the stamina to do what you've called me to do in spite of the pressures trying to distract me and call me away from my duties.
Amen.

per·sist·ence

Compassionate Giving

poor, noun.

1. those lacking wealth; the poverty-stricken.
2. the undernourished and lean.
3. those deserving of pity; the unhappy and wretched ones.
4. *Biblical:* the needy, the widows, the orphans, the oppressed.
5. *Personal:* the destitute among you for whom God calls you to provide support.

poor

In Joppa there was a follower named Tabitha. She was always doing good things for people and had given much to the poor.
Acts 9:36 CEV

words *to live by*

You noticed her around town in her dilapidated sedan and long, shaggy hair. She was just a part of the landscape that you ignored because she had nothing to do with you. She did not run in your circles. She had no style. But one day she entered your church, Bible in hand and with a hungry look that had nothing to do with the fact she'd had no breakfast that morning. She began to turn your social world upside down as she dug into your heart. She was poor and a child of God and wanted to be your friend.

The poor in the Bible are the weak, afflicted, and humble of spirit. They are the needy ones, whether financially disabled, mentally distressed, or socially oppressed. The Hebrew word *ani* signifies one who "lives from day to day and is socially defenseless, being subject to oppression." The godly are to protect and deliver the afflicted *ani* poor. In the ancient world, the majority of people were poor, that is, materially deprived. God commands that society protect them. The Old Testament prophets cried out vehemently on behalf of the poor. Jesus' main ministry was aimed at the poor, and he voluntarily became poor. It is a good thing for all Christians to love the poor and be active on their behalf. At the same time, the poor should not be looked down on nor shown prejudice in any church.

A wealthy tax collector, Zacchaeus, found faith in Jesus and immediately wanted to take care of the poor. Jesus did not demand it, nor even suggest it. "Look, Lord!" Zacchaeus said. "Here and now I give half of my possessions to the poor, and if I have cheated anybody out of anything, I will pay back four times the amount."

The human tendency is to keep them poor. It's a kind of power to have others always indebted to you, dependent upon your largesse. You may have to fight the tendency to keep the poor in "their place." How simple and nonthreatening it is to toss money at them. The poor can be an object of your false piety. It helps if you allow the Lord to reveal your spiritual poverty, the ways in which your own heart is starving for purity and is hungry for love. Think through whether your material possessions or social status have blinded you in any way to your spiritual state.

Your first priority is doing what you can for the believers in your

It's probably too late for us to revert to a simple life style, but we are aiming instead at a controlled one—controlled by God and by a conscious self-discipline motivated by a sense of responsibility to this needy world.
LORRIE LUTZ

Compassionate Giving

> Whenever we have the opportunity, we should do good to everyone, especially to our Christian brothers and sisters.
>
> Galatians 6:10 NLT

church and community who have needs you can help fulfill. Beyond that, ask God to give you a love for the destitute and enlarge your heart's desire to meet their real needs. Assess your actions toward those who have less than you—in your neighborhood, church, and community. Compare how you treat your wealthier friends and family. Would you welcome them anywhere, any time, especially into your home, openly and unashamed?

The poor are anyone low, reduced, helpless, or weak, but especially those with few material resources. In ministering to the poor, you're more effective if you're aware of your own poverty of soul and spirit. God's Word expounds on treatment of the poor. God delights in your helping the poor with the motive of love. You must treat them impartially, without prejudice, and consider them friends.

words
to live by

Things you might not know about *poor*:

❶ The saying "poor as a church mouse" goes back to seventeenth-century England. Churches in centuries past offered lean pickings to mice, since churches were used only for services and prayer, unlike churches today with well-stocked kitchens.

❶ Americans, only 6 percent of the world, consume 35 percent of the resources. The U.S. ranks below the top ten Western nations in the percentage of Gross National Product donated to needy countries. However, the tax structure encourages private donations. Charities in the U.S. collect more than $26 billion annually.

After you've given your tithe and God brings someone to your attention who has a legitimate need, at this point, you give your offering.
LARRY BURKETT

God help me to do for the poor as much as if I knew I was to live only this day.
GEORGE WHITEFIELD

When you give a feast, invite the poor, the maimed, the lame, the blind. And you will be blessed.
Luke 14:13 NKJV

God, open my eyes to the needs around me
that I can fulfill. Put in my heart the name
of someone I need to reach out to.
Amen.

poor

pow·er, noun.

1. the force of energy used to do work.
2. the ability to act or produce an effect.
3. authority, command, dominion.
4. **Biblical:** control over all creation that belongs only to God.
5. **Personal:** the God-given strength to fulfill his will for your life.

pow·er

I pray that out of his glorious riches he may strengthen you with power through his Spirit in your inner being, so that Christ may dwell in your hearts through faith.

Ephesians 3:16 NIV

When your loved ones become incapacitated and can't take care of their own affairs, someone needs to take control. Someone needs power to work on their behalf to look out for their best interests. Such authority is called by its legal term, *power of attorney*. The ideal is that the one with this power will use it to accomplish the loved ones' desires as if they were in a position to express it.

You need power in all kinds of circumstances, to take care of yourself and accomplish good things for other people. You need power to live the Christian life and to do God's will.

In the New Testament, the Greek word for *power* is *dunamis*, from which comes the word *dynamite*, and refers to "strength," "might," and "the ability to perform"—in God who has absolute, unrestricted power, in the gospel, in miracles or "mighty deeds," in angels, in his Word, and in Jesus.

A Vigorous Strength

words
to live by

Jesus' disciples Peter and John knew exactly the source of their power for their ministry. They didn't dare ascribe their abilities to their own talents or efforts. When questioned about the mighty deeds they had done, they witnessed to the power of the name of Jesus. God's *dunamis* power and grace gave the apostles confidence, courage, and stamina for the great challenge of starting the Christian church.

Very few people know how to use power in a good way. The powerful need balances and restraints to keep them from abusing others for their own selfish purposes. Power for them means doing what they want, when they want, no matter how it hurts others. The power that comes from God also brings choices about your steward-ship and your responsibility before him, and on how you will use that strength and those abilities he gives. God's power enables you to control yourself in times of tempta-tion and testing and to do what pleases him, what he shows you day by day he wants of you.

God's *dunamis* power enables you to tell others about Jesus in such a way that they believe. He empowers you to be filled with hope, to be saved from your sins, and to overcome the evil one. In fact, God delights in revealing himself to others around you by shining his power through the cracks of your weaknesses.

Reality #1: God pursues a love relationship with you.
Reality #2: God invites you to join him in his work.
Reality #3: God speaks to his people.
Reality #4: You experience God as you obey him.
HENRY BLACKABY

When you recognize your need for God's power, it should draw you closer

ce mercy love faith goodness truth freedom hope
rgiveness peace humble holiness obey repent perfect submit
serve fellowship comforter transformed noble character church

A Vigorous Strength

You will receive power when the Holy Spirit has come upon you; and you shall be My witnesses both in Jerusalem, and in all Judea and Samaria, and even to the remotest part of the earth.
Acts 1:8 NASB

to him, to draw sustenance from him. You need God's power in sorrow, in making decisions, when wounded by relationships, when exhausted, when depressed, and when tempted. There's never a moment when you don't need God's power. The power of God through the Holy Spirit is available to every believer in Jesus Christ. Ask him to fill you and to control you each and every day. Release yourself to his power in a moment of surrender.

God's Word says that you have been given power by God. God's power and greatness are revealed in the Scriptures and through his work in your life. When you sense a lack of power in your life, seek God for his. Spiritual power helps you accomplish God's will. Possessing power reveals important things about yourself. It can be used to do good or as brute force.

words
to live by

Things you might not know about *power:*

❶ Your electric company is called a "power company." The company bills you for the amount of kilowatts used. A watt is a measurement of power (one joule per second).

❶ According to sociologists, women in all ages have discovered ways to exert their feminine influence and power within the legal and cultural restraints and structures of their times. Women have used the power of their mind, will, and creativity to capitalize on any advantages afforded them.

Spiritual power will always vary in direct proportion to spiritual dedication.
JAMES STEWART

Being powerful is like being a lady. If you have to tell people you are, you aren't.
MARGARET THATCHER

God's Spirit doesn't make cowards out of us. The Spirit gives us power, love, and self-control.
2 Timothy 1:7 CEV

God, how I need your power to live this life. Fill me with your Spirit. Infuse me with strength to accomplish your will today. Amen.

p o w · e r

grace mercy love faith goodness truth freedom hope
rgiveness peace humble holiness obey repent perfect submit
serve fellowship comforter transformed noble character church

Applause for Heaven

praise, noun.

1. as in a eulogy.
2. acclamation, applause.
3. recommendation, hearty approval.
4. **Biblical:** homage and adoration rendered to a high and holy God.
5. **Personal:** public or private audible gratitude for who God is and all he has done for you.

praise

All together now—applause for God! Sing songs to the tune of his glory, set glory to the rhythms of his praise.
Psalm 66:1–2
THE MESSAGE

Suppose you go to church one Lord's Day and the sanctuary is filled with balloons and crepe streamers. The congregation is wearing formals and tuxedos. The sounds of air horns and smells of cake and fresh popped corn fill the air. It's like party time. And then the room's filled with glorious music and beautiful singing as God's people unite in worship and praise.

Every worship service should have some element of a party spirit, of anticipation, of exuberant praise offered to God: "Jubilate Deo!" You leave behind the burdens of work and all your things to do and praise the Lord. It's all right to exert energy into your enjoyment of God. Praise opens the huge golden doors into his throne room of grace. Jesus, the one that makes it possible for you to be there, motions to you to enter. You are in the presence of the almighty God, the King of kings, the Lord of lords.

words
to live by

The Hebrew word for *praise, yadah,* means "to give thanks," also "to confess." Most often, God is the object of *yadah* praise, usually in public worship, where members of a congregation corporately affirm and renew their relationship with him. *Yadah* praise's vista is both vertical and horizontal, embracing all creation as well as heaven. *Yadah* praise is to revere the King with extended hands.

When Mary, mother of Jesus, went to visit her relative Elizabeth, she burst out in glorious praise for the wonder of what God was going to do through her. Mary's song is called the "Magnificat," because that's the opening word in the Latin Vulgate translation that means "glorifies." Mary celebrated God's might, holiness, and mercy.

Praise and worship seem to be a universal need. Every tribe or culture worships something. If they don't worship the one true God, they will worship someone else. They will boast of someone's greatness, to give expression to their desires to exalt and honor another. You were created to be devoted to, to honor, and to praise a divine being.

God may be praised with voices and instruments. Praise finds expression through testimonies and prayers too. Praise may be public or private. Worship is something you do, not just something you say. Sing, shout, proclaim, bless, celebrate—give your total being. You may not be able to sing or play "Hallelujah," but you can give God excellent praise.

Let's praise His name! He is holy, He is almighty. He is love. He brings hope, forgiveness, heart cleansing, peace, and power.
LUCILLE M. LAW

ness grace mercy love faith goodness truth freedom hope
rgiveness peace humble holiness obey repent perfect submit
serve fellowship comforter transformed noble character church

Applause for Heaven

Sing to the LORD, you who do what is right; honest people should praise him. Praise the Lord on the harp; make music for him on a ten-stringed lyre.

Psalm 33:1–2 NCV

Praise worship is getting caught up in God's glory, majesty, power, and love, and enjoying him for who he is.

Praise God for how he created you, the unique and special person that you are. Praise God for all the material blessings he has given you. Praise God for being your protection, for providing a place of safety, for delivering you from your enemies. Praise God for taking care of you in your everyday struggles. You may feel helpless at times, but you need never be hopeless. Your God is able to deliver. Praise God for his power to create, to change the course of nature, to change the most stubborn heart. Praise God for being your strength, your joy, and your salvation.

🔒

Praise springs from the delight of knowing God and saying to him, "I love you!" Praise is one of the things you can do for God that you know brings him pleasure. Praise is jubilation, the carefree spirit of thanksgiving and worship to God. Praise can be part of a joyous festivity, even in the church service.

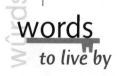

words
to live by

Things you might not know about *praise:*

❶ The Hebrew word *halal* is the source of "hallelujah," an expression of praise in every language on earth. *Hallelujah* is generally translated "praise the Lord." The more technical interpretation for the Hebrew form is "let us praise Yah," *Yah* being the shortened version of *Yahweh*, the Jewish name for God.

❶ Internet groups for women in public ministry reveal that many struggle with how to deal with praise. Corrie ten Boom offered the praise back to God, where it belonged.

Singing a hymn, a Scripture song, or a Sunday school chorus helps me say things to God that He enjoys hearing.
JAN JOHNSON

The origin of praise is the leaping of the Spirit within us, the outpouring of God's Spirit upon us.
THEODORE W. JENNINGS

All who worship the LORD, now praise him!
Psalm 22:23 CEV

God, I praise you for your mighty goodness. I praise you for your power and love. I praise you for all you've done for me, are doing now, and will do in the future.
Amen.

praise

ess grace mercy love faith goodness truth freedom hope
rgiveness peace humble holiness obey repent perfect submit
serve fellowship comforter transformed noble character church

A Sober Calling

prayer, noun.

1. any verbal contact with God.
2. a humble entreaty.
3. a memorial or petition.
4. **Biblical:** the means of contact and fellowship with God.
5. **Personal:** the constant, alert communication between you and God.

p r a y e r

I pray also that the eyes of your heart may be enlightened in order that you may know the hope to which he has called you, the riches of his glorious inheritance in the saints.
Ephesians 1:18 NIV

Every day is crammed with something—medical appointments, carpools, customers to appease, piles of laundry. Busyness can be like an addictive drug that you can't live without. Yet the distractions and details that seem so urgent at the moment steal the important things from you. The bustle of hurriedness can keep you from keeping in close communion with God through prayer.

The Bible is a book of prayers. Out of 667 recorded prayers, there are 454 documented answers. Samples of these answered prayers include Isaiah 38:5, Luke 1:13, and Hosea 14:2, 4–7. But even more important than the answers to prayer is the fact that prayer itself opens up communication and fosters fellowship between you and God.

Most people think of prayer as pleading for God to do something. And it's so easy to say, "I'll pray for you." It's like saying, "Bless you, child," or "So long." Then

words
to live by

you forget you said it, but there was another opportunity for being in God's presence and spending time with him. People in trouble pray, begging and bargaining, then go on with life as usual when the crisis passes. But for those who desire to know God personally, who run to him because they miss him, not just to demand something, prayer is more than an emergency line. Prayer is your private time to be with God, your best friend. When is the best time for prayer? Old Testament Jews often set aside three daily periods of prayer: 9:00 a.m., 12:00 noon, and 3:00 p.m. At least three times a day they remembered God. God's Word says to pray constantly. How is that possible?

Any system, schedule, or catalyst that gets you consciously into God's presence will work. All day long be alert to opportunities to commune, to fellowship with the Lord. Quick prayers on the road establish contact. Watching and reading the news every day can activate interaction with God about world events. Use that time for intercession and enjoyment of his presence. Praying before meals, even in restaurants, provides another time to remember that God is with you, to tell him how much you love him. You become more intent with prayer when you love God, when you're aware of his promises and bring their claims to him, and when time with him is precious. The Christian life is a relationship, not a ritual.

Faithfulness and persistence are key to an effective prayer life, and they are the

O the pure delight of a single hour that before thy throne I spend. When I kneel in prayer, and with thee, my God, I commune as friend with friend!

FANNY CROSBY

A Sober Calling

We always pray that God will show you everything he wants you to do and that you may have all the wisdom and understanding that his Spirit gives.
Colossians 1:9 CEV

biggest challenge. To pray constantly, to make prayer an everyday, every moment habit, is the goal of the serious Christian. Prayer is keeping your attention on God for every matter that concerns your life. Prayer is being spiritually alert—clear-minded and self-controlled—despite the multitudes of temptations and diversions. When you're clear-minded, you stay sober—rational, sensible, disciplined, earnest, watchful, wide-awake—abstaining from anything that would make you out of control. Prayer demands serious thinking. This is necessary for prayer in desperate situations, as well as prayer in ordinary moments. Prayer is attentiveness to the most important Person in your life.

🔒

In the middle of busyness, take time to be tenacious with prayer. Anytime, anywhere is a good time to pray—at the mall, in the car, while cooking dinner. It's only through stopping your mind's race of thoughts and getting alert to God that true prayer happens. Prayer is most important as quality time with God, not getting something from him. Prayer is being conscious of God's presence, enjoying him, talking with him.

words
to live by

etcetera . . .

Things you might not know about *prayer:*

❶ A green or brown predatory insect has been called the *praying mantis* since at least 1706. Also called the praying locust, this beneficial insect that eats destructive bugs in the garden is so named because of the position in which it holds its forelegs, as if in prayer.

❶ The longest prayer in the Bible is Nehemiah 9:5–37: at 1,096 words (TLB), it takes six and a half minutes to read. "Lord, save me" is the shortest prayer (Matthew 14:30) and takes a second.

Without prayer, our relationship with God is one-sided; he communicates with us through his Word, but we don't return the favor.
JOAN LLOYD GUEST

I learned the power of prayer when I became willing to step off my spiritual pedestal, humble myself, and admit my need for prayer.
EVELYN CHRISTIANSON

I get down on my knees before the Father, this magnificent Father who parcels out all heaven and earth.
Ephesians 3:14–15
THE MESSAGE

God, keep prompting me to come close to you, to talk to you about everything. I love communion with you. Please help me to stay in your presence while I'm rushing around.
Amen.

prayer

pride, noun.

1. an overly high opinion of oneself.
2. indulgence in self-glory.
3. vanity that craves admiration and applause.
4. **Biblical:** the arrogance of heart that God hates.
5. **Personal:** being so full of yourself that there's no room for God.

pride

Your clothes reveal something about yourself. They represent your gender, your culture, your social status, your style, and your personality. Clothes are part of how you announce yourself to your world. The intensity of attention—the dominance you give to your clothes, makeup, and jewelry—provides clues to how much trouble you may have with pride.

The mention of pride in God's Word is usually negative, the opposite of humility. Pride equates with arrogance. Pride claims, "I earned this and I deserve this," which described the nation of Israel. A prideful person is one who is puffed up with her own importance, feeling better than others. Pride is the high opinion that small souls entertain of themselves.

Because King Nebuchadnezzar refused to deal with his pride after being warned by Daniel, he went insane for a while, lost his kingdom, and was driven away to live like a wild animal.

The wicked are too proud to turn to you or even think about you. . . . In their hearts they say, "Nothing can hurt us! We'll always be happy and free from trouble."
Psalm 10:4, 6 CEV

High Esteem for Small Souls

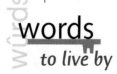

words
to live by

Some pride is necessary to function as a productive human being. If you didn't like yourself at all, if you didn't find some satisfaction in your abilities, you would never give yourself in positive ways to the world. It's not wrong to do well and be proud of it. Pride has a place in your life if it's under the lordship of Jesus Christ. The danger comes when you place all your confidence and sense of worth in your human accomplishments. The problem arises when personal pride aims to gain status over others, to put others down in order to raise yourself up. Misplaced pride is so self-focused, so self-consumed, that there's no room for others, including God.

If you are one of those who have a strong ministry of giving out all the time and of meeting other people's needs, you may have a hard time recognizing a problem with pride. After all, everything you do is done for God, supposedly. It takes a powerful enlightenment from God's Spirit to reveal how much of what you do is motivated by your own human need and how much leaves God out of it. A sign of this can be how hard it is for you to receive from others or how easily you resent the lack of gratitude from the ones you serve.

Some believe that inordinate pride is connected with or is the actual core cause of almost every other sin. The remedy is to confess your pride problem to God and to a trustworthy friend. Allow the Holy Spirit to deal with your areas of pride. Give Jesus

> I prayed that He would give me the wisdom and direction I needed to help other people, but I would not confess how desperately needy and empty I was feeling.
> CHRISTINE DALLMAN

ness grace mercy love faith goodness truth freedom hope
rgiveness peace humble holiness obey repent perfect submit
serve fellowship comforter transformed noble character church

your whole heart every day. Learn how to laugh at your mistakes, and learn from your failures—don't let them drag you down endlessly, for that, too, is pride.

Make a daily practice of releasing every success, accomplishment, and piece of prosperity back to God, to whom it belongs. Welcome an opportunity for some humble, invisible position of service, and do it gladly. Memorize verses that help keep your perspective, such as Isaiah 66:2, John 3:30, and James 4:6. Determine how to do all your boasting "in the Lord." Know the joy of being liberated from the burden of maintaining an image for pride's sake.

Live in harmony with each other. Don't try to act important, but enjoy the company of ordinary people. And don't think you know it all!
Romans 12:16 NLT

🔒

Pride is an attempt to appear in a more superior light than is true, mainly because you disregard the gifts and grace of God. Negative pride either disregards God or forgets him, and dismisses him from some area of your life. There's no room for him in the pride place.

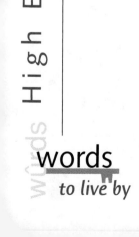

words
to live by

etcetera . . .

Things you might not know about *pride:*

❶ While some lionesses in a pride of lions hunt, the other lionesses "baby-sit" the cubs. But all the selfish pride belongs to the dominant males, who eat first, then let the lionesses and cubs scramble for leftovers.

❶ Theologians claim pride, the first of the seven deadly or capital sins, is the original or master sin from which all sins flow. When you do what you want and not what God wants, you're open to any sin. The deadly sins are pride, covetousness, lust, anger, gluttony, envy, and sloth.

Instead of focusing on our own accomplishments and desires, we need to do what will glorify God.
CHRISTIN DITCHFIELD

If pride is acting as though we have no need of God, then anything that breeds self-sufficiency or deadens us to our need of God is a potential culprit.
DAVID W. HENDERSON

Pride leads to destruction; humility leads to honor.
Proverbs 18:12 CEV

God, I offer you my heart right now. Guide me away from everything that's centered on my own selfish pride. I need your help with this. I'm too blind to do it myself.
Amen.

pride

No Longer an Enemy

rec·on·cil·i·a·tion, noun.

1. renewal of friendship.
2. resolving a dispute.
3. establishment of harmony.
4. **Biblical:** the satisfaction of God's just wrath against sinners.
5. **Personal:** offering the first steps to peace after estrangement.

rec·on·cil·i·a·tion

If you are about to place your gift on the altar and remember that someone is angry with you, leave your gift there in front of the altar. Make peace with that person, then come back and offer your gift to God.
Matthew 5:23–24 CEV

The apostle Paul could be strict. Very strict. The missionary team fell apart because Paul insisted young Mark not go with them again. The lad had failed to stick it out on the first journey, and that perturbed Paul. But a few years later, Paul asked for Mark to be brought to him in prison. Who will you want close to you in your last days? Paul wanted Mark.

The Greek word for *reconciliation, katallasso,* denotes "to change from enmity to friendship." The Greek *apokatallasso* means "to reconcile completely" so as to remove all enmity, leaving no impediment to unity and peace. God the Father initiated such a reconciliation with sinners through his Son's sacrificial death. By filling you with love, the Holy Spirit makes the ministry of reconciliation possible as he works through you to others.

One of the most dramatic scenes of reconciliation in the Bible, besides the story of the prodigal son, is Esau's running

words
to live by

to meet his brother, Jacob, after experiencing the pain of deceit and betrayal. He threw his arms around his neck and kissed him as a sign he'd been forgiven.

Reconciliation is the process of changing something to adjust to a standard—for one's own convenience and to make the day smoother. For instance, you adjust your watch to a time signal, reconciling the watch to a time standard, so you can keep appointments and get to work when you should. You reconcile your checkbook to the bank's record of your account so you won't be overdrawn. But reconciliation is rarely that easy when it comes to the emotional mess of restoring relationships. The process can cause much agony before the sweet relief.

You are hurt most by those you love. They know you well enough to strike the heart. The eventual desire for reconciliation signifies there was a prior good relationship worth saving. Here are some suggested steps to work through to find possible reconciliation.

Write down the reasons for the estrangement. Think through your main motive for wanting reconciliation. God's motive for reconciling with you is love. Pray for this person to experience God's blessings. Pray for yourself, for the power of the Holy Spirit to do what you must. Start the process of letting go of the hurt and anger.

Think through whether you can trust again, become vulnerable again, in order to grow and change. Seek to forgive, no matter

> Despite inevitable disappointments, with God's grace, our relationships can still flourish. It's vital to attempt reconciliation if there's ever to be any healing.
> EILEEN SILVA KINDIG

No Longer an Enemy

If anyone is in Christ, he is a new creation; the old has gone, the new has come!
2 Corinthians 5:17
NIV

who is most to blame in your opinion. Shoulder your part of the responsibility. Swallow your pride, say, "I'm sorry," but realize that apologizing may not be enough. A follow-up of acts of kindness and striving to restore trust might be required.

Don't expect instant closeness. How much time it takes depends on the level of the hurt, the length of distance, and how much each values the friendship. Practice patience and figure out a level of understanding. Stay connected through any opening available to you. Work it through to full restoration, through all the bumps along the way. If the other person refuses to go the distance with you, bless her and let her go.

❶

Reconciliation in relationships occurs when a state of enmity and estrangement is replaced by peace and fellowship. God's Word encourages you to take those first few steps to make that happen, whether with a friend, family member, or fellow believer. However, that's not easy to do—you need the power and aid of the Holy Spirit.

words
to live by

etcetera . . .

Things you might not know about *reconciliation:*

❶ The Victim-Offender Reconciliation Program (VORP) brings offenders face-to-face with the victims of their crimes through the assistance of a trained mediator. Offenders begin a process of restitution for their actions, and victims speak their minds and feelings, contributing to the healing process of the victim.

❶ Many communities have a Family Reconciliation Service (FRS) devoted to maintaining the family as a unit and preventing the out-of-home placement of adolescents.

Friendship redeems. It pulls broken parts together and offers healing.
MADELEINE L'ENGLE

Reconciliation is the personal reunion of people who were alienated but belong together. It is the beginning of a new journey together.
LEWIS B. SMEDES

I am giving you a new command. You must love each other, just as I have loved you.
John 13:34 CEV

God, there are people around me who are estranged. I intercede now on their behalf and ask that you show me what I can do to help them heal.
Amen.

rec·on·cil·i·a·tion

181

A Rude Awakening

re·jec·tion, noun.

1. discarding as defective.
2. refusing to recognize.
3. repudiation.
4. **Biblical:** the disdainful refusal to accept the treasured offer of God's love.
5. **Personal:** the feeling of being cast away as worthless.

re·jec·tion

All these God-signs he had given them and they still didn't get it, still wouldn't trust him.
John 12:37
THE MESSAGE

words
to live by

Rejection hurts.

Passed over by the cute boys at the dance. Turned down by the college of your choice. Your heart broken by the guy of your dreams. Family members or friends turn their back on you. Layoffs or the humiliation of getting fired. Any of these scenes of rejection and an inner voice berates: "You are worthless."

The Bible is honest about God and rejection. God will not force anyone to do his will, so he sometimes must resort to rejection himself. Although God chose Saul to be king, Saul's disobedience and disregard of sacred things caused him to be rejected. Esau endured rejection because he didn't take his birthright seriously. God created beings with freedom of choice, so God also faces the possibility of rejection. A common theme in the book of Psalms expresses the agony of the *feelings* of being rejected. Psalms also affirms that God never rejects those who cast their hope on him.

Jesus knew he would face rejection when he entered this world. It was even predicted. But rejection did not prevent Jesus from doing what he came here to do. Nor should encountering rejection deter you from your appointed destiny, but that's easier said than done.

Sometimes criticism seems like rejection. Criticism is pointing out mistakes, even though it hurts and cuts, without abandoning the project or person. True criticism is meant to improve, not spurn. Criticism can be a teacher, especially if you have hints as to why. At other times, you can try to be honest and get judgment back that feels like rejection. Rejection or acceptance of Jesus is a test of where a person stands with the one true God. All believers share in some ways in the rejection that Christ endures.

Rejection is disapproval after examination, a refusal to accept. Rejection has to do with freedom of choice— you can reject whomever you please. Others may do the same to you through whatever it is you offer them. When you're on the receiving end, rejection brings pain, anger, and frustration. In a world where rejection is possible and probable, you must learn to live with it. But rejection can't alter facts. You are God's child. You have immense worth in his sight. Who you are can't be governed by the responses of people around you.

Few people handle rejection well. You want to be valued and understood. But you can use rejection to deepen your trust in God. The biggest challenge is to regain your sense of confidence that you're worth some-

You must want to enough. Enough to take all the rejections, enough to pay the price of disappointment and discouragement while you are learning.
PHYLLIS WHITNEY

ness grace mercy love faith goodness truth freedom hope
orgiveness peace humble holiness obey repent perfect submit
serve fellowship comforter transformed noble character church

A Rude Awakening

If you were of the world, the world would love its own. . . . but I chose you out of the world.
John 15:19 NKJV

thing to him. Don't give in to the temptation to hide out from everyone when you've been rejected. Bring to God all your sense of being cast away. The God who has known rejection, the Jesus who was rejected for your sake, can sympathize with your struggles. Work to find a larger perspective beyond your own hurt, to God's overriding purpose. It may not change the rejection, but you will be able to better cope with it.

❶

You feel rejection when you aren't wanted or when you're snubbed. Rejection brings pain. Rejection is being discarded as worthless. Try to learn from experiences of rejection. Grow in your relationship with God, remembering you're his precious daughter. Because God gave humans freedom of choice, some will reject best friends and spouses and siblings. But the good part is that God will never reject someone who puts her hope in him.

words
to live by

Things you might not know about *rejection:*

❶ Some large U.S. cities provide commercial companies called Rejection Services. You keep their number handy in your purse or wallet and when you don't want to reject someone to their face, you give them that number as yours. When they call, the Rejection Service provides a prerecorded rejection message.

❶ Madeline L'Engle's book *A Wrinkle in Time* was turned down twenty-nine times before she found a publisher. C. S. Lewis received over eight hundred rejections before he sold a single piece of writing.

Like [Jesus], you will experience that strange feeling of rejection by God himself, when you cry out, "Father, Father, why have you forsaken me?"
CATHERINE DOHERTY

Character consists of what you do on the third or fourth tries.
JAMES MICHENER

He was in the world, and though the world was made through him, the world did not recognize him.
John 1:10 NIV

God, in the midst of feeling rejection, I cry out to you. Give me strength to get past this pain that would make me feel otherwise. Lead me to your better future. Amen.

r · e · j · e · c · t · i · o · n

The One-Another Rules

re·la·tion·ship, noun.

1. connections by blood or marriage.
2. affiliations, alliances, associations.
3. kinships.
4. ***Biblical:*** all the important people to love who constitute "your neighbor."
5. ***Personal:*** the test for love and discipleship for every believer.

re·la·tion·ship

A wife cherishes her husband. A mother sides with her child. A daughter nurses an aging parent. A grandmother leaves a heritage. Sisters become friends, and friends grow close as sisters. Relationships define family and community. Relationships spawn churches, cities, and nations. Relationships provide motivation for fighting evil and doing good and learning love because you know these people well enough to care what happens to them.

This is how everyone will recognize that you are my disciples—when they see the love you have for each other.
John 13:35
THE MESSAGE

Your relationships consume the largest part of your Christian discipleship. That's why Jesus narrowed down all the commandments to two: "Love the Lord your God with all your heart and with all your soul and with all your mind" and "Love your neighbor as yourself" (Matthew 22:37–39). How you do relationships proves how full you are of God's love and how closely you follow Jesus.

words
to live by

So much of God's Word deals with how to do relationships—the importance of forgiveness, living in peace, showing respect, exhorting the lazy, refraining from vengeance. The list goes on and on. Often these words are used when addressing relationships: "one another"—as in "be devoted to one another," "honor one another," "live in harmony with one another," and, most of all, "love one another." God instituted relationships, right from the beginning, for your health and well-being. The Bible also acknowledges that there are limits in doing perfect relationships, but you must continually try.

Moses found out the hard way that it's risky trying to reconcile contentious relationships close to you, when you are imperfect yourself. Few people are open to criticism, and certainly no one wants to be corrected by someone who hasn't gotten her own life together. However, in order for relationships in family, among friends, and in the fellowship of believers to work, imperfect people must exhort another in love.

Everybody wants people to love them, to understand them, to stick by them, but few do the tough work it takes to make relationships last. Only the truly committed struggle through the inevitable hurts. Only those with high spiritual motivations strive to love others more than themselves. Someone said, "Good warm relationships, like a good warm fire, need continual stoking." Relationships don't just happen. Someone has to make a conscious effort to persevere or relationships stagnate or die.

It is only when we appreciate what a gift our women friends are that we'll make the effort to overcome the obstacles that threaten friendship's survival.
DEE BRESTIN

...ness grace mercy love faith goodness truth freedom hope
orgiveness peace humble holiness obey repent perfect submit
serve fellowship comforter transformed noble character church

The One-Another Rules

Every relationship in the vicinity of a Christian constitutes a "kingdom relationship." Your interaction with God and the people around you and over you become spiritual priorities because they're important to God and the display of his kingdom here on earth. Who gets the prime attention depends on what the Lord's teaching you from his Word and the needs of the day, with God always asking for first place.

Knowing God, being filled with his Spirit, and obeying his Word won't guarantee all your relationships will be right. But it will mean you'll have a growing desire that they be. There're only two relationships you can count on—your relationship with God and your relationships with people you're determined to love no matter what.

> If you fall, your friend can help you up. But if you fall without having a friend nearby, you are really in trouble.
> **Ecclesiastes 4:10** CEV

Relationships are a test of your Christian commitment and your greatest challenge. Though everyone wants some, few fight to keep them. You have to battle for time, attention, and priority to commit to your relationships and to love God's way. As long as you're trying and you keep bringing them to God, you're not flunking your test.

words
to live by

Things you might not know about *relationships*:

❶ Sociological studies show women's friendships are deeper and more plentiful than men's. But today's women may find it more difficult to maintain friendships because of time, hurts, risks. Yet, a *Family Circle* survey of 15,000 women revealed that 69 percent would rather talk to best friends than husbands when unhappy.

❶ One recent study of college students' use of counseling services at Kansas State University showed that the percentage of students seeking help for relationship problems rose from 34 percent in 1989 to 60 percent in 2001.

You may like someone because of who they are; but you love them because of who you are.
NEIL ANDERSON

It isn't the ones who die with the most toys who win. It's those who've loved their families well and know the joy of having that love returned.
RUTH HALEY BURTON

The commandment that God has given us is: "Love God and love each other!"
1 John 4:21 CEV

God, show me who needs my love and attention today. Give me insight in what to do to reach out to someone who's been hurt or wounded by me.
Amen.

r·e·l·a·t·i·o·n·s·h·i·p

189

Sorrow-Based Action

re·pent, verb.

1. to feel sorrow or regret for past conduct.
2. to change one's mind.
3. to desire to reverse one's life direction.
4. **Biblical:** to turn completely from sin and walk in obedience toward God.
5. **Personal:** to be so sorry for the wrong you've done that, with God's help, you change.

re·pent

God can use sorrow in our lives to help us turn away from sin and seek salvation. We will never regret that kind of sorrow.
2 Corinthians 7:10 NLT

It started out as teasing. "Did you see those lips?" Peggy whispered.

"You've heard of Botox, haven't you?" her friend replied.

"You mean they're phony?"

Her friend gave her a smug grin. "It's just a rumor."

From there it grew. Peggy and her friend invented more stories until the woman became a joke to their whole crowd. One day the woman committed suicide. Their teasing turned to grief. They wondered how much they were to blame. They felt a strong need to repent.

The Hebrew word *shuv* for *repent* means "to turn around" or "return," which emphasizes strong movement and focus of direction. Repentance is a turning away from sin and toward God, as in the parable of the Prodigal Son. Jesus' main

words
to live by

message was to call individuals to repent, and he got upset when his call for repentance was ignored. Repentance is a requisite of salvation and was meant to go to all the world. Jesus' disciples preached repentance too.

Job may be the first person in the Bible to repent. The people of Ninevah repented when Jonah preached, and King David humbly confessed and repented in Psalm 51. Saul of Tarsus repented on the road to Damascus, and John the Baptist offered baptism for repentance in a very public way.

Some folks feel it's worth it to siphon up pleasure as long as they can and endure the pain that comes along with it. Those caught in sins that yield devastating consequences may regret what they suffer, but not enough to quit doing the sin. Others will only admit to doing wrong. If and when they're caught, they're only sorry they were exposed. Some experience great grief because of their sins but never repent, so their sorrow does them no spiritual good. Their remorse is self-indulgent. Some show the false appearance of repentance in order to generate sympathy for oneself. It's called "damage control."

Repentance is a decision of the will to quit thoughts, words, or deeds that are wrong. You grieve over your sin because you see it as God sees it. If the pain of your sin turns you to God and motivates you to make changes, you have repented. True repentance brings about a radically altered life, including changed relationships. You seek to prevent returning to that sin.

Remorse is the echo of a lost virtue, one of those terrible moments when the wheel of passion stands suddenly still.
EDWARD ROBERT BULWER-LYTTON

191

Sorrow-Based Action

Jesus answered and said to them, "Those who are well have no need of a physician, but those who are sick. I have not come to call the righteous, but sinners, to repentance."
Luke 5:31–32 NKJV

Sin leads you into deceit and lies. Repentance heads you into truth. Knowing how to repent should be mastered by every believer. Repentance starts with confession. The Greek words *homo* and *legeo* combined mean "to say the same thing"; that is, confession is agreeing with God that what you did was wrong. To repent or turn from sin means to go in a different direction. Find an accountability partner. Make changes in your habits, and don't assume you only repent once. You don't become perfect when you receive God's forgiveness. Repentance of sins on a daily basis keeps your relationship with God fresh, alive, and free from guilt.

Thank God that he allows repentance rather than your having to live under guilt forever. Heaven rejoices with you when you repent.

❶

Repentance is basic to Christian faith, is necessary to come to Christ, and is an important part of daily discipleship. To repent is to agree with God about your sin and change your behavior. How to know if you really did repent: your actions match the sorrow in your heart. Any brave soul who turns from her sin and turns toward God will bring thunderous approval from heaven.

words
to live by

etcetera . . .

Things you might not know about *repent*:

❶ Repent is found forty-six times in the Old Testament, and twenty-eight of those times it is God who does the repenting, or changing his mind.

❶ Signs of repentance are found in 2 Corinthians 7:9–11. They include regret and godly sorrow that leads to salvation and visible change. The change involves eager diligence in doing right and anger at the shame of one's sin and the dishonor it brought to God.

It is impossible for a person to live without sinning. There are so many things to draw away the heart and affections of people from God.
DWIGHT L. MOODY

Repentance is an act of the will, a willingness to turn away from sin.
BRUCE JONES

Turn to the Lord!
He can still be found.
Call out to God!
He is near.
Isaiah 55:6 CEV

God, I repent today, making no excuses. Out of my sin I turned away from you and your mighty love and chose a shameful act. Forgive me and help me turn around and run the other way.
Amen.

re • pent

Also Known As

rep·u·ta·tion, noun.

1. a general estimation of a person or place.
2. fame; public distinction.
3. character; good name.
4. **Biblical:** the name by which you are known by God.
5. **Personal:** the opinion of others in how you represent the name of Jesus.

rep·u·ta·tion

Avoid foolish and ignorant disputes, knowing that they generate strife. And a servant of the Lord must not quarrel but be gentle to all, able to teach, patient, in humility correcting those who are in opposition.
2 Timothy 2:23–25
NKJV

You guarantee a product. You research what others say about a hairdresser. You check the studies on car performance. You consider the source when someone tells you a shabby old house is a hundred years old. You watch for signs of courtesy and consideration from the sales department. A customer defaults on a credit commitment. All these actions have to do with building a reputation.

The Hebrew word *shem* for *reputation* means "name" or "renown, fame." Sometimes a person's name reveals the essence of who she is. Names as reputation in the Bible include Peter, "the rock"; John and James, "sons of thunder"; and Barnabas, "son of encouragement." Reputation and character, his very identity, is emphasized by all the names of God. *Shem* is a worthier goal when honoring God's name and furthering his reputation and fame.

words
to live by

Queen Esther's cousin Mordecai didn't seek honor, but he gained his reputation from consistent integrity. A woman named Tabitha built her reputation by "doing good and helping the poor."

It's so common to hear "I'm tired of being known as a goody two-shoes," and then an outrageous act is committed to prove how easily you can blow a reputation. It seems of no account that a good reputation takes such a long time to build and can be lost by one bad choice.

Your reputation is judged by other people, what they think and say about you. You can develop a reputation on your abilities and your talent. Your reputation could advance your name and fame into the nation or world. Reputation matters, but it isn't necessarily what's true about you. Reputation is a perception of what you seem to be. Reputation doesn't always assess your inner character. The most solid reputation is built from the inside out, by truth and integrity in the inward parts of you.

Opinions can be formed through quick and slanted impressions. That's why gossip and slander are especially vile weapons, just because they tear down reputations. However, character defines who a person really is. Character is who you are under fire, in a crisis, or in the daily humdrum of family life. Character is what you are before God.

There's another issue to consider about reputation. You must determine how much it matters what other people think. For

> Cautious, careful people, always casting about to preserve their reputations, can never effect a reform.
> SUSAN B. ANTHONY

.ness grace mercy love faith goodness truth freedom hope
orgiveness peace humble holiness obey repent perfect submit
serve fellowship comforter transformed noble character church

Also Known As

> Be careful how you live among your unbelieving neighbors. Even if they accuse you of doing wrong, they will see your honorable behavior, and they will believe and give honor to God when he comes to judge the world.
>
> 1 Peter 2 :12 NLT

instance, Jesus warned that it's not always good that everybody speaks well of you because you probably aren't letting your Christian stance show enough. The apostle Paul placed serving Christ above pleasing others. Jesus himself did not pay much attention to what others thought of him in doing God's will as his highest priority. On the other hand, "A good name is to be more desirable than great riches; to be esteemed is better than silver and gold" (Proverbs 22:1). The key is Jesus—his will and your relationship to him in each and every situation. You want to guard his reputation. The highest goal of the Christian disciple is to display the character of Jesus and to be known by reputation as one of his.

There are times to risk even your reputation in order to please Jesus.

🔑

"Shem" means not only reputation, but also fame. Reputation is the public perception of who you are. A public reputation can deceive. You could put on a good show of outward appearances, but inwardly be something else. Character includes your motives and private choices. It's honorable to seek a good reputation, but in your spiritual walk you want to please God.

words *to live by*

etcetera . . .

Things you might not know about *reputation:*

❶ In a court of law, reputation is the character imputed to a person in the community in which he or she lives. It is admissible in evidence when character is part of the issue, or when such reputation is otherwise part of the case.

❶ A Reputation Manager helps Internet users discern reliability for the two million Web sites available. A Web site is judged by brand, that is, by its known qualities, and by reputation, the advice of other users who know the site's quality.

Build your reputation by helping other people build theirs.
ANTHONY J. D'ANGELO

Begin somewhere; you cannot build a reputation on what you intend to do.
LIZ SMITH

A sterling reputation is better than striking it rich; a gracious spirit is better than money in the bank.
Proverbs 22:1
THE MESSAGE

God, help me build my reputation from the inside out. I want to be purified in my motives and make all my choices from inward integrity. Most of all, I want to please you.
Amen.

r · e · p · u · t · a · t · i · o · n

re·spon·si·bil·i·ty, noun.

1. a thing or person one is answerable for.
2. obligation, duty.
3. being subject to an authority.
4. *Biblical:* accountability to the supreme ruler of the universe.
5. *Personal:* taking care of the persons and tasks appointed to you by God.

re · spon · si · bil · i · ty

Make a careful exploration of . . . the work you have been given, and then sink yourself into that. Each of you must take responsibility for doing the creative best you can with your own life.
Galatians 6:4–5
THE MESSAGE

An employee is promoted. A graduating student takes her first teaching job. A paycheck is received. A man and woman get married. A child is born. What do these scenarios have in common? Responsibility.

The Hebrew words *nasa* or *nacah* for *responsibility* mean "to lift," "to bear up," "to carry." The Greek *hupodikos* adds the aspect of being accountable as unto God. Responsibility to God presumes there's a supreme moral ruler of the universe to whom you're accountable, who sees all and knows all. You take on a great responsibility once you own a Bible, to know what it says and follow its dictates. It is to the God of the Bible you are responsible for how you live your life. It is your responsibility to repent of your sins and prepare yourself to one day be accountable before him for every thought, word, and deed.

At times you may want to run from

words
to live by

responsibility and its burdens. Some characters in the Bible felt that way. Jonah booked passage in the opposite direction of Ninevah. Young John Mark deserted Paul and Barnabas in Asia and headed for the security of home.

You live in an era when it's encouraged to be more concerned with your rights than your responsibility. That can distort relationships and skew discernment about choices. The key is to serve and make decisions by the law of love. God's Word emphasizes meeting someone else's needs before your own.

Responsibility is an obligation made before God to a person or project, making sure that some expectation is met. Responsibility makes no excuses nor does it blame others for neglecting duty. Responsibility is at the heart of following Christ. The Christian faith is a responsibility religion. You are responsible to God for every thought, word, and action. You are responsible for those the Lord appoints to be under your care. But you need God's love to serve them. "Feed my lambs, take care of my sheep," Jesus repeated to Peter three times for emphasis. You are responsible to love your neighbor as yourself. A couple of other responsibilities are to pay your debts and obey the commandments.

The weight of responsibility can be overpowering. However, sometimes you may have a tendency to take on too much responsibility and become overwhelmed with other people's problems. Jesus promised that his yoke is easy and his burden is light.

> When we stand before Christ, He will not ask us if we received everything we had coming to us. But He will reward us for how well we fulfilled our responsibilities.
> NEIL ANDERSON

It's important to determine exactly what responsibility has been appointed to you by the Lord and what is for someone else to do. You do what you can. Someone else does what she can. The results are left to God. In fact, you can place each facet of your responsibility in his hands while actively, faithfully tending to your part.

Responsibility can develop your strength and character or it can burn you out. Responsibility comes with God-appointed tasks and skills for your ministry in the fellowship of believers. The best way to fulfill each responsibility is as though you're doing it for Christ, in the power of God's Spirit.

The day is coming when God will judge all of us. . . . And so, each of us must give an account to God for what we do.
Romans 14:10, 12
CEV

Responsibility is taking care of an obligation given you by God. It's to him you are accountable for people and projects. But you must make sure those burdens were divinely appointed to you and not just taken on yourself. What he gives you he will also empower you to do. You love your neighbor by the way you take care of your responsibility.

words
to live by

Things you might not know about *responsibility:*

❶ Physicians for Social Responsibility is using its professional influence to protect human health from threats of nuclear war and general gun violence. It brings pressures to bear on countries and companies who have responsibility in dispersing guns and weapons of mass destruction.

❷ San Diego State University offers a Responsibility course that focuses on personal, community, and global responsibilities. The students learn to define responsibility, recognize its importance, notice how it changes throughout a person's lifetime, and foresee responsibilities to future generations.

Action springs not from thought, but from a readiness for responsibility.
DIETRICH BONHOFFER

Sorting out the matters for which we are responsible and relaxing about the unchangeables . . . liberates us to act within God's will.
WONDA LAYTON

Guard what has been entrusted to your care.
1 Timothy 6:20 NIV

God, teach me how to complete each of my responsibilities. Help me be trustworthy and persistent. May others see that it makes a difference that I serve in Jesus' name. Amen.

re·spon·si·bil·i·ty

...ness grace mercy love faith goodness truth freedom hope
orgiveness peace humble holiness obey repent perfect submit
serve fellowship comforter transformed noble character church

Precious Offering

sac·ri·fice, verb.

1. to give up something cherished.
2. to consecrate, to dedicate.
3. to surrender to obtain some advantage.
4. **Biblical:** to give an offering to God for forgiveness of sin or to please him.
5. **Personal:** to surrender what you'd like to keep, in order to achieve God's will.

sac·ri·fice

You are also a group of holy priests, and with the help of Jesus Christ you will offer sacrifices that please God.
1 Peter 2:5 CEV

Sure, you'll give away the battered, bright orange sofa any day. No big deal to part with secondhand goods. But that's not even close to sacrificial giving. A true sacrifice is giving up a treasure with love and a willing heart for the sake of another who will enjoy it more. Sacrifice is offering your brand-new leather couch.

Sacrifice is at the heart of the Gospel. The ultimate sacrifice was Christ's death on the cross. The body of the believer is to be presented to God as a living sacrifice. There's also the privilege of sacrifice in doing good to others. The Hebrew *qorban* for *sacrifice* means "that which one brings near to God or the altar." You bring your sacrifice near to God and surrender it to him.

A poor widow sacrificed two pennies, and Jesus was so impressed he pointed it out to a crowd of witnesses. For most people, this would be no sacrifice at all. This

words
to live by

illustrates the point that no one should judge another's sacrifice, nor compare it with her own.

In the marketplace, when you want to make a purchase and aren't willing to pay the price listed, you ask the owner to make the sacrifice. Among the powerful, when they want to preserve their position, they may force the sacrifice of the lives of others. Sacrifices made to God are done voluntarily and at your cost. You don't offer a sacrifice to God in order to change his mind or force him to do something for you. That's superstition at play. You sacrifice because he has asked something of you in order to bring about a holy work in you or through you. That's obedience. But anything you lose is all gain as he blesses your life with abundance.

Following Jesus is not for the fainthearted.

You may sacrifice something truly major, like your health. For the apostles this meant being flogged because they preached about Jesus. Or you could sacrifice your wealth. The rich young ruler discovered this was too high a price for him to pay. Or you might have to give up support or approval for the sake of Christ or alter your plans for the future. On the other hand, you may sacrifice in much smaller ways, such as offering treasures and trinkets that you might like to keep, but you feel a special prompting by God's Spirit

> Dedicate some of your life to others. . . . It will be an exhilarating experience because it is an intense effort applied toward a meaningful end.
> THOMAS DOOLEY

 less grace mercy love faith goodness truth freedom hope
orgiveness peace humble holiness obey repent perfect submit
serve fellowship comforter transformed noble character church

Precious Offering

Take your every-
day, ordinary life—
your sleeping, eat-
ing, going-to-work,
and walking-around
life—and place it
before God as
an offering.
Romans 12:1
THE MESSAGE

that someone else will enjoy them more.
And you can offer him a sacrifice of praise.
You can count any and every circumstance
"all joy," because somehow God is in it with
you.

Perhaps you may never sacrifice anything, but you should be willing to do so. A
heart that's set to sacrifice mode fills a life
with exuberant worship, cheerful service,
clear-sighted vision, and vitality for doing
God's will as you rid yourself of loving this
world and the things in it too much.

*Sacrifice is surrendering something of
intrinsic value in order to accomplish a
spiritual good. A willingness to sacrifice
anything of yourself or your possessions
frees you from being too tied to this
world. Any kind of sacrifice for God's
sake is voluntary. He might nudge about
giving up something, but will allow you
to choose. Sacrifice is at the heart of
Christianity because of what Jesus did
on the cross.*

words
to live by

Things you might not know about *sacrifice*:

❶ The animals selected for Old Testament sacrifices were from the ordinary staples of diet among the Hebrews. This expressed gratitude to God for his blessings. Presenting these offerings symbolized consecration to God.

❷ In baseball, a sacrifice play occurs when the batter intentionally hits the ball in such a manner as to advance teammates on the bases, while the batter is thrown out. A sacrifice play is a purposeful out for the betterment of the team.

The important thing is this: to be able at any moment to sacrifice what we are for what we could become.
CHARLES DU BOS

Humility must always be the portion of anyone who receives acclaim earned in the blood of followers and the sacrifices of friends.
DWIGHT D. EISENHOWER

Everything else is worthless when compared with the priceless gain of knowing Christ Jesus my Lord.
Philippians 3:8 NLT

God, I give myself and all I own to you. Let me know what you would have me to do and for whom. I love you more than all of these.
Amen.

sac·ri·fice

God's Generous Grace

sal·va·tion, noun.

1. deliverance from evil.
2. redemption.
3. liberation from danger or ruin.
4. **Biblical:** Jesus' sacrificial death to deliver sinners from God's just wrath.
5. **Personal:** the love gift of God offered to you when you trust Jesus and repent of your sins.

sal·va·tion

What a feeling of joy when you see the pictures—loved ones reunited after survival of a disaster. Such a glad reunion when everyone is home and safe. In the same way, God longs to be restored to every person he created. He wants everyone to come to his open arms, to receive deliverance from the ravages of sin through the sacrificial plan of his salvation. The best time to receive salvation, if you haven't already, is right now.

God did not appoint us to wrath, but to obtain salvation through our Lord Jesus Christ, who died for us.
I Thessalonians 5:9–10 NKJV

The Greek *soteria* for *salvation* means "deliverance" and "preservation." Salvation comes through material, temporal deliverance from danger and apprehension, but the most important salvation brings God's eternal deliverance to those who accept his conditions of repentance of sin and faith in Jesus Christ. The gospel message exhorts you to confess Jesus as your Savior and Lord. At the point of salvation, God begins to work in you to help you become like Jesus.

<u>words</u>
to live by

Zacchaeus believed Jesus was who he claimed to be, and then he demonstrated that belief by voluntary restitution for the wrongs he'd done. Jesus declared that salvation was his. Zacchaeus didn't receive an exhortation that salvation would come sometime in the future if he toed the line and lived a sinless life from then on. He received that gift instantly.

Many people believe they can please God and get to heaven by doing lots of good things to counteract the bad things they do. Some think salvation comes through self-denial, rituals, laws, or self-inflicted suffering. But God's Word teaches that everyone's heart left on its own is deceitful and holds great potential for evil. Nothing that anyone attempts to do on her own will ever change this fact. Even some who admit the wickedness of humanity don't consider the plight to be so bad as to require a savior. Others discount biblical truth about God and what he says with an "I don't believe he's that way" and live in any way they want. That's like trying to do your job and ignoring your boss's every instruction. That's like insisting on seeing the Queen of England and ignoring every rule of protocol. God is in charge of how people make peace with him, of how they get to know him, and of the conditions for receiving his offer of salvation. The Bible says that no one comes to God except through Jesus.

The most common steps to salvation begin with hearing the Gospel: God the Father loves you, and God the Son died for your sins. When you believe that simple but

> The Christian hope is grounded in the conviction that Jesus Christ, the incarnate Son of God, died on the cross for our sins and rose again.
> BRUCE NICHOLLS

...less grace mercy love faith goodness truth freedom hope
..rgiveness peace humble holiness obey repent perfect submit
..erve fellowship comforter transformed noble character church

God's Generous Grace

I am not ashamed of the gospel, for it is the power of God for salvation to everyone who believes, to the Jew first and also to the Greek.

Romans 1:16 NASB

incredible truth, you will want to confess your sin in private and Jesus in public. The completion happens when God the Spirit comes to live inside you.

Your salvation provides numerous benefits. Your salvation is like a helmet of protection from mortal spiritual snares, saving you from soul-threatening attacks because you now belong to God. This helmet covers your head and mind, the most critical part of you, where spiritual battles are won or lost.

You have not yet experienced all the rewards of your salvation. You will praise God for your salvation for all eternity.

Many ideas are offered as to how to be friends with God and get to heaven. The only true way is the one he offers— repenting of your sins and accepting Christ's death on your behalf. The gift of your salvation provides many benefits. You learn as you walk with Christ more of what it means, its power and its joy.

words
to live by

Things you might not know about *salvation:*

❶ It cost between $5,000 and $10,000 to save lost hikers missing for two days in a snowstorm on Oregon's Mount Hood. Debate ensued concerning who should pay for the extensive and costly search. More than one hundred volunteers considered their efforts a love offering in hopes of saving the hikers.

❶ The Salvation Army was founded in 1865 in England by William Booth to minister to the poor and to bring the message of God's salvation to the masses. Members are called Salvationists.

Only a God who suffers can save us.
DIETRICH BONHOEFFER

We live "in between" Christ's resurrection and the resurrection of all things.
GEORGE CAREY

Only Jesus has the power to save! His name is the only one in all the world that can save anyone.
Acts 4:12 CEV

God, I love you and praise you for your gift of salvation that makes me spiritually alive and free to walk forgiven in this world today.
Amen.

sal · va · tion

grace mercy love faith goodness truth freedom hope
rgiveness peace humble holiness obey repent perfect submit
erve fellowship comforter transformed noble character church

Devotion to Duty

ser·vant, noun.

1. an employee who performs domestic services.
2. a person devoted to another.
3. an assistant in a trade or vocation.
4. **Biblical:** one who suffers on behalf of others.
5. **Personal:** giving cheerful service to God in the most menial of tasks.

ser·vant

> Whoever wants to become great among you must serve the rest of you like a servant.
> Matthew 20:26 NCV

The huge auditorium is filled with the rich and famous. TV cameras roll as a star-studded cast of presenters come one by one to the podium. You hold your breath as the final announcement is made: "And the Servant of the Year Award goes to . . ."

You'll probably never hear that declaration. Servants don't get special honors at fancy affairs. One reason is that what they do is unobtrusive, behind the scenes. Servants aren't showy. The most common word used to describe a Christian in the New Testament was the term *servant*. It was said of Mary, mother of Jesus, of the apostle Paul, of deaconess Phoebe, of Tychicus, an associate of Paul's, of evangelist Epaphras, of James, the brother of Jesus, and of the apostle Peter. They wore the title with pride. To be a servant of Jesus is to follow his own example. And although the Greek *doulos* for *servant* signifies "in bondage," Jesus accepted that

words
to live by

limitation. He is the greatest example of servanthood.

A servant does what is asked of her by the boss. The servant must be actively doing her duty, even when the boss isn't present. Attitude matters. Christ's servant must be peaceful, helpful. The faithful and wise servant is given much responsibility. You are to be Jesus' personal servant, which means you are to follow him wherever he leads. However, he prefers to call you a friend. The key to becoming great in God's kingdom is to aim at servanthood.

Few aspire to be a servant. It's servile labor with low pay, the bottom rung of the work force. There's no affluence or sense of achievement connected with such a position. It's tough being a servant for a living. It's even more difficult having a servant's heart in the family or church. Someone else sets the agenda. Someone else assigns the tasks. You will not always know how your role fits in with the Master's plan. Your success belongs to the Master—he gets the credit. You need the Lord's supernatural help to become a servant.

To be Christ's servant is a great honor. His servants serve with the strength God provides and are not offended if not given recognition. You serve by doing the nasty jobs, such as scrubbing toilets or vacuuming nurseries. You serve by responding to needs as you know them in your church or community. In order to be a better servant, you may need some kind of training. Some acts

> I don't claim anything of the work. It is his work. I am like a little pencil in his hand. He does the thinking. He does the writing. The pencil has nothing to do with it.
> MOTHER TERESA

we ... g. ..... merey love faith goodness truth freedom hope
urgiveness peace humble holiness obey repent perfect submit
serve fellowship comforter transformed noble character church

Devotion to Duty

You are free, but still you are God's servants, and you must not use your freedom as an excuse for doing wrong.
I Peter 2:16 CEV

of service involve particular tasks like helping the elderly, aiding the poor, caring for children. Nobody's born knowing how to be an effective servant.

You can know you're doing the will of God by engaging in acts of servanthood, especially if you do them with a willing and cheerful spirit. But always remember in this case that the Master cares more about you as a person than the work you do for him. Even so, the ultimate reward for any child of God is a simple "Well done, good and faithful servant."

It's not easy being a servant, either outside or inside the church. A servant of Jesus Christ follows his own example. A servant of Jesus Christ has discovered the highest calling in God's kingdom. You can serve while mopping floors or dishing out food at the homeless shelter. The important attitude is a willing, cheerful spirit. The greatest reward of Christ's servant is to hear his "well done."

words
to live by

etcetera . . .

Things you might not know about *servant:*

❶ In northwestern Europe in the 1800s, people often circulated between households as servants. It was quite common for men and women in late adolescence to leave home and to spend a few years working in other people's houses as servants and nannies before marriage.

❶ Voice of Calvary Ministries, founded in 1964 in Mississippi, is headed by a "board of servants" that deals with housing needs, health care, nutrition, education, voter registration, and start-up assistance for small business co-ops to break the cycle of poverty that traps the poor.

[Jesus] came to serve. To give. To pour out Himself for others. He expects the same of us.
MARK R. LITTLETON

The true test of a servant is if I act like one when I am treated like one.
BILL GOTHARD

He who is greatest among you shall be your servant.
Matthew 23:11 NKJV

God, make out of me an effective servant for you. I want to have a servant's heart. Forgive me for resenting menial tasks. Help me do everything I do in the name of Jesus and for his sake.
Amen.

ser·vant

213

...ace mercy love faith goodness truth freedom hope
...rgiveness peace humble holiness obey repent perfect submit
...erve fellowship comforter transformed noble character church

Bent and Defective

sin, noun.

1. immorality; iniquity.
2. trespass; offense.
3. any lack of holiness.
4. **Biblical:** a condition of estrangement from God.
5. **Personal:** giving in to the desires of the heart in rebellion against God.

s i n

Some plants are beautiful but deadly. Animals may seem cuddly, but some are dangerous. So many things in life look appealing but contain hidden traps. You may desire a thing that's harmful, or be lured to a place that's life-threatening. Sin is like that. The pleasures of sin come accompanied with soundtracks of sweet, alluring voices and scents of sensual summer nights. Sin needs to also include signs that say AVOID, DO NOT PASS BY, TURN AWAY.

All have sinned; all fall short of God's glorious standard.
Romans 3:23 NLT

The Hebrew word for *sin, awen,* also means "vanity" and "sorrow." There's much sorrow in the vanities of sin. Sin is moral worthlessness. Sin entertains for a moment and reaps consequences for years. The word *'awon* means "to be bent, bowed down, twisted, perverted." *'Awon* portrays sin as a perversion of life, intent, truth; a twisting into error. Every heart is prone to willful disobedience. Sin is missing God's mark.

words
to live by

Everyone in town knew what kind of woman she was. Her sins were legend. How dare she approach a man like Jesus and make such a fool of herself. She fell at his feet and poured expensive perfume all over him. Jesus considered it an act of love. He proclaimed her sins forgiven.

Sin is such an old-fashioned concept to many. Some tease and joke about the sins that the Lord takes so seriously. Too often, the difference between right and wrong depends on the flow of political correctness or social acceptability, rather than on God's Word. Even those who know they've done wrong tend to make excuses and to blame someone else. They call it "a complex situation," anything except "sin." Sin always has a name. It's called pride, envy, or anger. It also goes by greed, lust, or lying.

In order to deal with sin, you must confess it, make it an effort of constant prayer, repent of it, and flee from its influences. Be accountable to someone you trust when you're tempted. Meditate on and memorize God's Word on related topics. Open your heart to the Holy Spirit's cleansing work.

Sin separates. Sin spoils relationships between people. All sin is rooted in selfishness—placing one's own desires and wishes ahead of the needs of others and of the will of God. You can get so caught up in your own importance, or so busy, that you forget to take account of your daily sin factor, until you fall flat.

[The author of John 1] was saying, in effect, "Make it your aim 'not' to sin." As I thought about this, I realized that deep within my heart my real aim was not to sin "very much."
JERRY BRIDGES

idness grace mercy love faith goodness truth freedom hope
orgiveness peace humble holiness obey repent perfect submit
serve fellowship comforter transformed noble character church

Bent and Defective

Believers must come to the place of honestly admitting that in themselves nothing good and holy exists. Jesus knows your sin struggles and took the brunt of every one of your sins on the cross. His death conquered sin's fatality for the forgiven believer.

Even in your bleakest hour of failure, you must remember you're only one confession away from forgiveness and cleansing. No sin is so horrible that the blood shed by Jesus can't take care of it. When you know you're forgiven, you can boldly claim with millions of others, "There is now no condemnation for those who are in Christ Jesus" (Romans 8:1 NASB).

If we admit our sins—make a clean breast of them—he won't let us down.
1 John 1:9
THE MESSAGE

Sin is a twisting of the right way, a perversion of the heart. It is moral failure toward both God and people. Sin is awful in its action and consequences. Everybody has some. You need to know what sins you're prone to and take preventative measures to keep from falling. Jesus' sacrificial death saves believers from the full brunt of sin. When you confess and repent, God tosses your sin into the sea.

words
to live by

Things you might not know about *sin*:

❶ Type the word *sin* into an Internet search engine and you pull up more than 36,000,000 hits. Everyone knows about sin, has an opinion about it, and wants to talk about it. Many have recorded their words of wisdom for the world to see.

❶ The term *sin* comes from God himself. A Hebrew word for sin, *chatta't*, is used in Genesis 4:7: "If you do not do what is right, sin is crouching at your door; it desires to have you, but you must master it" (NIV).

I had spent my life trying to be a star and a hero for Jesus, when He is the Hero and the Star, and I am simply to worship Him.
ANN KIEMEL ANDERSON

God's Son had to die to bring humanity back to God. That one fact shows the full seriousness of human sin.
DAVID GILLETT

I am obedient to God's standards with my mind, but I am obedient to sin's standards with my corrupt nature.
Romans 7:25
GOD'S WORD

God, help me choose the right way today. Guide me by your Word and the power of your Holy Spirit. Help me pay attention to the consequences.
Amen.

sin

A Voluntary Surrender

sub·mit, verb.

1. to be subject to some condition or process.
2. to give up or abandon.
3. to bend to another's will.
4. **Biblical:** to obey God by obeying the leaders over you.
5. **Personal:** to defer voluntarily to the wishes of someone in authority over you.

s u b · m i t

Leonard Bernstein was once asked which musical instrument was the hardest to play. After a moment the conductor replied, "The second fiddle. I can get plenty of first violinists, but to find someone who will submit to play second fiddle with enthusiasm—that's a problem. Without second fiddle, we have no harmony."

Playing second fiddle demands submission to first fiddles, for the good of the performance. Submission is yielding for a larger purpose.

The Greek *hupeiko* means "retire," "withdraw," "yield," as in "Obey your leaders and submit to their authority" (Hebrews 13:17 NIV). The Greek *hupotasso* means "to subordinate," "to yield to one's admonition or advice." It also means "to bear up under" and "to support." A simple illustration is how the leg of a table supports the tabletop so that it can support something else. To submit is to

Submit to one another out of reverence for Christ.
Ephesians 5:21 NIV

words
to live by

voluntarily yield to the decisions of another because of your reverence for God and obedience to his Word.

For Christians, submission is a lifestyle choice. You submit to God's Word. You submit to God's righteousness. You submit to the government, to one another in the family unit, to Jesus as head of the church, to God's discipline, to church leadership, and to your boss.

Submission contradicts your instincts. You may feel the drive to scratch and compete to get ahead. To submit reeks of weakness or forced obedience that's contrary to your well-being. It's not in you to do what you're told. That's because submission strikes the heart of your old nature, and that's exactly why it's critical to God. Whether you submit or not reveals your true commitment to him.

But submission isn't an absolute law with no limitations. To submit is a volunteer position. To submit is a choice because you perceive this action will produce the best possible spiritual results. To never submit to anyone about anything is to forgo helpful input or partnerships. You can never live up to your full potential or receive certain protections that another's support can bring.

You can't submit to God if you don't listen to him. Prayer and study of his Word are essential to learn when and how to submit. Discipleship happens while you're trying to get to that place of submission, the crucifixion of the stubborn will—not to destroy, but to transform it. Submission is

> Surrender involves a willingness to accept someone else's terms. In our relationship with God, it means letting go of our own "terms" and embracing God's.
> ADAM R. HOLZ

uness grace mercy love faith goodness truth freedom hope
orgiveness peace humble holiness obey repent perfect submit
serve fellowship comforter transformed noble character church

A Voluntary Surrender

yielding the right of way to someone else, to prevent constant frustration and anger in relationships. To submit is to willingly accept someone else's terms. It's the prayer of relinquishment—"not my will, but yours be done."

Relationships are about power struggles. To submit is to show deference to others; respect them. Submission means placing yourself under orders of an authority or peer. Submission is Christlike meekness, as you release the burden of pride and pretense. Submission is a spiritual act of obedience to God.

Submission is not a sign of weakness; rather, it is just the opposite. It shows your self-discipline and strength of character. Jesus is your example. His life is described as "reverent submission." That's a eulogy to inspire you.

Long ago those women who worshiped God and put their hope in him made themselves beautiful by putting their husbands first.
1 Peter 3:5 CEV

Human nature bristles at the thought of others telling you what to do. However, biblical submission is voluntary; it can never be forced. It's your choice. Submission sometimes means playing second fiddle for the good of the whole orchestra. You learn the art of submission by submitting each day to God as you study his Word and pray for guidance.

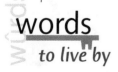

words
to live by

Things you might not know about *submit:*

❶ The coronation ceremony for British monarchs includes replacing Saint Edward's Crown with the Imperial Crown, but only after the king or queen submits to the King of Kings. After this pledge of allegiance to God, he or she then rises to take the reigns of the kingdom.

❶ Submitting a manuscript for publication requires courage. Rejection is possible, and you must defer to an editor's view of the value of your hard work.

Submission means I voluntarily limit what I might do naturally in this relationship in order to benefit you.
KEVIN A. MILLER

Submission leads to liberty, the liberty to be able to let go of the terrible weight and burden of always needing to get my own way.
RICHARD FOSTER

Place yourselves under each other's authority out of respect for Christ.
Ephesians 5:21
GOD'S WORD

God, help me know if I have a rebellious spirit. Show me where I need to submit to you. Teach me from your Word. Amen.

sub·mit

ness grace mercy love faith goodness truth freedom hope
orgiveness peace humble holiness obey repent perfect submit
serve fellowship comforter transformed noble character church

Blessed Achievement

suc·cess, noun.

1. a favorable course.
2. a prosperous termination.
3. good fortune.
4. **Biblical:** prosperity appointed by God out of his love.
5. **Personal:** accomplishing God's goals, using God's methods, in God's timing.

suc·cess

May he give you the desire of your heart and make all your plans succeed.
Psalm 20:4 NIV

A trapeze artist depends on incredible timing and competent cooperation of other circus performers to do her act. When the woman on the trapeze lets go of the "catcher" and turns to meet another performer to return her to the platform, there's a breathless second. She must grasp the trapeze or fall. In an instant she displays her abilities. Part of the entertainment involves the possibility that she'll miss the trapeze. If she succeeds, the crowd cheers. Success, or failure, isn't always so dramatic in other venues, or so public. Most spiritual success certainly isn't. It's much more hidden. But so important for God's kingdom.

The Hebrew word *tsaleach*, "to succeed, to prosper," is first found in Genesis 24:21. Abraham's servant was sent to find a wife for his son Isaac. Then he discovered Rebecca at the well. In the case of Joseph, Isaac's grandson, when the Lord provided success in everything he did in

words
to live by

the foreign land of Egypt, despite all the obstacles against him, people knew God had done it. Believers understand that all success comes from God, but full human effort is to be expended. The Lord was with King David in every success, but David had to fight the battles.

The common thinking is that worldly success in accumulating money, fame, prestige, or power comes from whom you know or from getting lucky or from cheating your way to the top. It's got to be done with push and shove and depending on the stars. The truth is, no matter the method used or the motivations behind it, no one could find success of any kind unless God allowed it. To ignore God's role in any blessing received in this life is foolish and ignorant. He who lifts up can also let down, according to his sovereign purposes.

It is all right to ask the Lord for success. Even better, it's good to ask God to help you reach his goals for your life.

Obedience to God's Word lines you up for his ordained success for you. Success always comes from the Lord, but he often uses people and other earthly resources to bring it about. Committing each step to the Lord eliminates impure motives and trivial diversions. You stick with the real goal he has in mind. Your part is to work as hard as you can. The Lord's part is to determine what kind of success you will have and when.

> Let us work as if success depended upon ourselves alone; but with heartfelt conviction that we are doing nothing and God everything.
> SAINT IGNATIUS OF LOYOLA

Blessed Achievement

I consider my life worth nothing to me, if only I may finish the race and complete the task the Lord Jesus has given me—the task of testifying to the gospel of God's grace.

Acts 20:24 NIV

God has given you several methods for success, including the prayers of Jesus. You may experience desperate spiritual battles. On the way to success, there may be numerous failures because of your weaknesses or getting it wrong or being passed over. But you will be able to persevere.

To be a success, you don't have to "have it all together." Spiritual success is the achievement of being all God wants you to be at any given moment, depending on him, seeking him out, and facing each challenge with his power.

No one can be a success unless God allows it. It's foolish not to acknowledge his part. His power and will gets you through all the harassments and discouragements along the way. Success will have lasting effect if it's part of God's goal and done God's way. Spiritual success is being who God wants you to be each step of the process.

words
to live by

Things you might not know about *success*:

❶ Looking at a newspaper in 1987 one could find President Reagan's name mentioned fifty-four times in nine different stories, Andy Rooney noted. But by 1989 his name was not mentioned even once. Even the highest success attainable in the country isn't lasting news.

❶ Studies have shown that in order for children to succeed in school, certain behaviors need to be changed: TV watching, interaction with family, manners, empathy for others. Studies confirm that problem-solving skills enhance children's chances for success in social skills and schoolwork.

Success in life is the equivalent of industry, knowledge, prudence, and perseverance, and the result of chance.
HENRY WARD BEECHER

What is it to succeed? It is to do the thing for which we were created.
CHARLES JEFFERSON

The God of heaven will give us success. We his servants will start rebuilding.
Nehemiah 2:20 NIV

God, what do you want me to do with my life? What are your goals for me? I want to accomplish your success for me, in your time, in your way. Amen.

s u c · c e s s

Purpose in the Pain

suf·fer·ing, noun.

1. the undergoing of pain or punishment.
2. adversity, affliction.
3. the torment of torture.
4. **Biblical:** what Jesus experienced for your sins.
5. **Personal:** mental, physical, or spiritual agony that accomplishes God's purpose in the yielded believer.

suf·fer·ing

Through the suffering of Jesus, God made him a perfect leader, one fit to bring them [God's children] into their salvation.
Hebrews 2:10 NLT

What if all pain disappeared? No headaches, no backaches, no stomachaches. But there'd also be no warning signals that you'd broken a bone or needed an appendectomy. Pain serves a purpose. Pain prevents ravages of the body when it loses sensation. Without the symptoms of pain, such ailments as ulcers, arthritis, and cavities can be destructive. Pain brings suffering, but not all suffering is bad. Suffering can produce a godly purpose.

The Hebrew word *yasar* suggests that suffering serves "to discipline," "to instruct," and "to chasten." The Book of Job tells of the suffering of a righteous person. When Job complained, God affirmed his sovereignty to do as he pleases to refine faith, teach trust, restore wholeness.

Some think all suffering is an illusion that can be overcome with mental gymnastics. Others consider suffering proof that you're being punished for some spe-

words
to live by

cific sin. Personal suffering sometimes causes loss of faith. The truth is that suffering is an agonizing reality for everyone at some time or other because of humanity's rebellion against God. Disobedience to the Lord of the universe caused havoc in the perfect order. The divinely appointed system got all twisted.

In suffering, you're prone to turn your attention to God, to learn who he is. Suffering can teach you obedience, as it did for Jesus. You learn to trust him and to obey him. God teaches and disciplines in love through suffering, and he corrects you or helps you to grow.

Some suffering is the first step in producing the character of Christ in you; therefore, it's a sign of the Lord's work in your life. Some suffering should bring you joy, if it accomplishes a purpose, such as confirming your faith or verifying your ministry.

Painful experiences help free you from illusions. You are forced to admit your limitations. You're made more aware of other people's suffering too. Knowing that others suffer as much or more than you do helps you endure your own.

It's common to think that your suffering is like no one else's and is in fact much worse. When you suffer, don't be ashamed to cry out to God in your anguish and to recommit yourself to the Lord in a deeper way. Push to do whatever good you can, however you can, especially to console other sufferers. Be alert

God had reasons behind my suffering, and learning some of them has made all the difference in the world. He has reasons for your suffering, too.
JONI EARECKSON TADA

Purpose in the Pain

When life gets really difficult, don't jump to the conclusion that God isn't on the job. Instead, be glad that you are in the very thick of what Christ experienced.

1 Peter 4:12–13
THE MESSAGE

to new spiritual truth he may be trying to tell you. God hears when you cry out to him in your suffering. Search out God's promises of comfort and hope. Constantly remind yourself that your suffering is temporary. In the scope of eternity, all suffering endures for just a little while.

The Christian message features a suffering God. The crucifixion of Jesus is central to the Christian faith, and God knows how to minister to your suffering. Some day, in heaven, there will be no suffering. Its purpose will have come to an end.

Suffering is any personal agony in mind, body, or spirit. Suffering entered the world because people refuse to acknowledge the sovereign rule of God in their hearts. Everyone, saints and sinners, suffers at some time. God sometimes allows pain and suffering as a form of chastisement. Suffering can be redeemed when you seek to understand a godly purpose through it.

words
to live by

Things you might not know about *suffering*:

❶ A century ago, "agony columns" in newspapers featured the sharing of personal sufferings. The columns were devoted to notices about looking for missing loved ones or any other personal struggles you wanted to make known.

❶ Russian astrophysicist Dr. Vladimir Khruinsky claims that getting rid of the moon would eliminate "hunger, want, and suffering around the world." He says the moon's gravitational pull gives earth a tilt that produces extreme weather patterns. By obliterating the moon, all suffering by natural disasters would be suspended.

God whispers to us in our pleasures, speaks in our conscience, but shouts in our pains; it is His megaphone to rouse a deaf world.
C. S. LEWIS

Although the world is full of suffering, it is full also of the overcoming of it.
HELEN KELLER

Those who suffer because that is God's will for them must entrust themselves to a faithful creator and continue to do what is good.
1 Peter 4:19
GOD'S WORD

God, into your hands I commit the pains and agonies all around me today. May you accomplish your powerful spiritual purpose in and through and in spite of it all.
Amen.

s u f · f e r · i n g

229

temp·ta·tion, noun.

1. an enticement to do wrong by promise of pleasure or gain.
2. an inviting attraction.
3. a provocation.
4. **Biblical:** tests provided by the world, your own flesh, and the devil to demonstrate obedience and devotion to God.
5. **Personal:** the lures to sin that teach you self-control.

temp·ta·tion

Temptation approaches women custom-made for them. Temptations arise in your need for nurturing relationships, in the midst of melancholy moods, in your desire for approval, in proving your worth, in combating loneliness, and in your hunger for love. Each temptation is designed to attract and capture just you. Playing upon your flaws and your lack of discipline, temptations slip between the gaps in your defenses.

The Greek word for *temptation* is *peirasmos:* "trials with a beneficial purpose and effect."

The scene in the Garden of Eden defines the dynamics of temptation. The Genesis 3 model reveals an attractive pleasure that is forbidden, yet promises fulfillment of a desire or need.

Jesus faced temptation. It tormented his spirit, but he didn't give in. That's why he is able to empathize with and help those who are tempted. God's Word warns to be watch-

Let us not be like others, who are asleep, but let us be alert and self-controlled.

I Thessalonians 5:6
NIV

words
to live by

ful at all times for temptation. God promises to make a way of escape from temptation. Overcoming temptation strengthens your character and faith.

Temptation for the believer is a deadly serious test. It's meant to be resisted—through a solid knowledge of God's Word, a habit of prayer, the flexing of strong values, and surrounding yourself with accountability witnesses.

Temptation arises from within, from uncontrolled appetites and passions that eventually rule over you. It's not sin to be tempted. But playing with temptation invites sin closer. Giving in to temptation is not inevitable. There's always some way to avoid it, to practice saying no.

Temptation begins in the thoughts. Temptation is someone or something that's enticing but doesn't belong to you and that causes you to ruminate until you're consumed with desire. The whisper of temptation can be heard farther than the loudest call of duty.

Here're some temptation overcomers. Review what you allow into your home through television, magazines, books, and other media. Never go places or be alone with people that might beckon you to sin. Someone once said, "The most dangerous place to be is where no one knows who you are." Write down all the consequences to yourself and those you care about if you should taste of this forbidden pleasure.

When tempted by the devil to doubt, resist with the Word. When tempted by the world to succumb to your ego, check out your devotional love for Him. When tempted by the flesh, the biological drives of the body, run.
CURTIS C. MITCHELL

ness grace mercy love faith goodness truth freedom hope
rgiveness peace humble holiness obey repent perfect submit
serve fellowship comforter transformed noble character church

Tested and Proved

How you deal with temptation reveals the firmness of or flaws in your character. Learn from your failures. Find new coping measures. Temptation usually involves some kind of deceit or betrayal to act it out. Make honesty, integrity, and openness with your loved ones a high priority.

Self-control is vigor, dominion, power, and strength to do what is right; a very strong will that's firmly held in rein. It has been said that self-control is a high form of worship before God.

Stand on God's Word as the absolute for right and wrong. Agree with God that this temptation would lead to sin. Name it and renounce it. Turn around and go the other way. Be prepared for a fight. Temptation rarely goes away the first time you resist. Give in to God instead.

Keep alert and pray. Otherwise temptation will overpower you. For though the spirit is willing enough, the body is weak!

Matthew 26:41 NLT

0

Temptations come to every child of God. The goal is to avoid temptation, so run from it—don't get as close as possible to see how much you can get away with. Dealing with temptation helps you practice self-control. It's a test of your faith and obedience. Practice the simple rules of overcoming temptation. Rely on the Holy Spirit to help you resist. If you do get entrapped, cry out to God to save you.

words
to live by

Things you might not know about *temptation:*

❶ Studies show that women are becoming addicted to pornography due to the temptations presented by easy access to the Internet. Counselors advise that women addicted to porn need professional therapy and a renewed sense of kinship with other women who understand.

❷ Companies know that even the thought of temptation sells. They market Temptation Perfume, Temptation Body Splash, Temptation Bubble Bath, Temptation Candles. And there are Chocolate Temptation Ultimate Truffles, as well as a book series called Harlequin Temptation.

When we indulge with delight in thoughts of forbidden things, we commit sin, even though our will has not yet consented to perform the deed.
JOHN OWEN

Lead us not into temptation, but deliver us from evil.
Matthew 6:13 KJV

What we are so convinced will bring us joy only brings sorrow. What we are so convinced will bring us pleasure only brings pain.
THOMAS À KEMPIS

God, show me the way out of my temptation. Keep me from evil and the evil one. Deliver me from my own sinful desires that would risk hurting my loved ones and cause me to lose what's dear and precious to me.
Amen.

t e m p · t a · t i o n

A Lifestyle Virtue

thank·ful·ness, noun.

1. consciousness of benefits that outweigh harms and hurts.
2. sense of favors received.
3. gratefulness.
4. **Biblical:** expressions of praise to God for divine mercies in forms of words and worship.
5. **Personal:** an attitude that helps overcome dark moods, dingy thoughts, and negative words.

thank·ful·ness

There's a beauty in thankfulness.

Though some tongues just love the taste of gossip, Christians have better uses for language than that. Don't talk dirty or silly. Thanksgiving is our dialect.
Ephesians 5:4
THE MESSAGE

The practice of being thankful relaxes and softens the face. It makes one courteous and generous of spirit. It improves your memory and deepens graciousness as you recall the blessings of the past. Thankfulness softens, lightens, and enhances your countenance and your world.

Giving God thanks sounds strange to those who depend solely on luck for things to turn out for them. If the mind's trapped on self and full of unbelief, it's impossible to consider the benevolence of a divine being. Yet, the earth's full of good things to enjoy. It's proper to be grateful for gifts, and it makes sense to seek out who it is that needs to be thanked.

Thanksgiving is a common theme in worship songs. The Hebrew word *todah* sometimes refers to the "thanksgiving

words
to live by

choir." One of the peace offerings in Leviticus was designated the thanksgiving offering. Thankfulness in public worship generates spirit-renewing gratitude to God for his mighty miracles and his salvation acts. Thankfulness helps exude joy toward God for who he is.

Daniel was carried off from his home into captivity as a boy. He lived in a foreign land, yet took the time and effort to find reasons to thank God at least three times a day. This habit never wavered, even at the risk of his own life.

To neglect expressing gratitude to God is a sin of omission. In fact, majoring in thankfulness is an antidote for futile thoughts and foolish hearts. Gratitude displaces whines and complaints. Thankfulness is a virtue that overrides and eliminates dark moods. Thankfulness overcomes worry, anger, and self-pity. Gratitude purifies a critical, judgmental spirit. To be thankful is a choice.

Give thanks with a grateful heart. Stir gratefulness with some practical helps. Write down a dozen things that fill you with gratitude. Record a moment when you know you met God today. Read aloud some of the thanksgiving chapters in the book of Psalms. Begin a thankfulness journal. Offer thanks to God for his goodness, even when nothing positive seems to be happening, as a declaration of trust. A thankful lifestyle is a sign of maturing discipleship.

> I learned that if I waited to *feel* grateful, nothing happened. It took sheer determination to stay on course when I didn't feel like it. However, as I persisted, genuine gratitude welled up within my heart.
> MADALENE HARRIS

Thank God for providing food and shelter, for providing a measure of peace,

ness grace mercy love faith goodness truth freedom hope
rgiveness peace humble holiness obey repent perfect submit
erve fellowship comforter transformed noble character church

A Lifestyle Virtue

Always be joyful. Keep on praying. No matter what happens, always be thankful, for this is God's will for you who belong to Christ Jesus.
I Thessalonians 5:16–18 NLT

for deliverance from dangers, for healing. Thank God in the midst of jarring phone calls, taking out the trash, shoveling snow, talking to customers. Make it a rhythm in your day, an exercise of the mind. Remember that if you have food in the refrigerator, clothes on your back, a roof overhead, and a place to sleep, you are richer than 75 percent of the people in this world. Thankfulness develops with creative thinking. An old Asian saying goes, "When eating a fruit, think of the person who planted the tree."

Thankfulness is a form of worship that recognizes God's divine mercies. Thankfulness works as a lifestyle to overcome constant negative thoughts. Make a conscious choice to transfer your focus to who God is and the gifts he provides. Gratitude transforms your perspective and crowds out depressive moods. Thankfulness can most easily be expressed in songs that generate a heart of gratitude.

words
to live by

Things you might not know about *thankfulness:*

❶ The first Thanksgiving was derived from an autumnal feast between Pilgrims and Massasoit Native Americans in 1621. The Massasoit provided five deer, and those gathered also ate duck, geese, turkey, fish, and corn.

❶ The old classic "Over the river and through the wood to Grandfather's house we go" was a Thanksgiving Day song: "Over the river and through the wood, trot fast, my dapple gray! Spring over the ground, like a hunting hound, for this is Thanksgiving Day."

Learn to be grateful for the moment—the cup of coffee with your mate or best friend, the beauty of the morning, the quiet evening with your family, the smell of the dew, and the fragrance of a rose.
HAROLD SALA

To look for the many little blessings is a choice we can all make.
LUCI SWINDOLL

Be thankful and praise the LORD as you enter his temple. The LORD is good! His love and faithfulness will last forever.
Psalm 100:4–5 CEV

God, thank you for my life today and everything in it. Most of all, thank you for your eternal goodness that makes me long to want to be with you and be like you. Amen.

thank · ful · ness

237

In His Care

trust, noun.

1. firm reliance on the ability or character of another.
2. a confidence in.
3. a dependence upon.
4. **Biblical:** the action of God's servants at his words.
5. **Personal:** complete reliance on God as being in charge of your present situation.

trust

Trust GOD from the bottom of your heart; don't try to figure out everything on your own.
Proverbs 3:5
THE MESSAGE

A friend impresses you with her poise and confidence. You've watched her as she deliberates choices, then always seems to decide wisely. Others are drawn to her to seek out advice. She handles emergencies with calm. You've never known her to ever tell a lie. She's up-front in all her dealings at home, in her job, in the community, even when she has to admit a mistake or apologize. She's the most level-headed woman you know. This is a woman you've learned to trust.

Trust is to be certain about, to have confidence in something or someone. Joseph had plenty of reason not to trust his brothers, so he tested them, to verify what was true in their hearts: "Bring your youngest brother to me," he said. When they bring Benjamin and are so solicitous for his care, Joseph finally believed he could trust them.

You can have misplaced trust. You can trust in riches. You can count on all

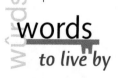

words
to live by

outcomes of your efforts being predictable. You can trust another person who's really deceiving you behind your back. You can trust your own self to save you. But God wants you to trust him instead. It is much safer to trust God than to trust any human.

You can tell when you're not trusting God: your heart's troubled or you feel out of control. The hard things you face in life can purge you of the tendency to rely on yourself. Trust is relying on God's person, his protection, his compassion, his purpose. Trust is committing your plight to the Judge of the universe and awaiting his final verdict. God's Word says you will never be put to shame nor disappointed if you put your whole trust in God. But it takes time and experiences to build complete trust in God.

Trust in God is a learned trait. Take little steps at a time. Trust in the Lord by delighting in him. Turn everything over to him. Trust that he knows what's going on, even if you don't. Pour out your heart to him, tell him everything in your heart and mind and in the situations around you. There are rewards for trust in God: he fills you with joy and peace. Trust in God should produce action, the doing of good deeds for others.

There are secret spiritual lessons concerning trust that are powerful to learn: it is in quietness of spirit and trust in God that you find strength to endure this life. When you exercise perfect trust you

We discover what we knew from the first—that we can trust God to forgive us our sins, and to forgive us our impenitence too, and to inspire us with the life and power of the Holy Ghost.
ROBERT WILLIAM DALE

In His Care

When I am afraid, I put my trust in you. O God, I praise your word. I trust in God, so why should I be afraid? What can mere mortals do to me?
Psalm 56:3–4 NLT

discover inner peace. And what a powerful moment when you finally realize you trust him. You know you're trusting God when you're quick to listen and respond to him. You check out the answers to your questions in his Book. You're in no hurry for your storms to get over. You aren't frantic about your problems, but patiently ride them through. Total trust doesn't happen until you've released the weight of all your hopes, dreams, and fears into his keeping.

🔑

Trust is believing in and depending on someone or something. The best source of trust in this world is God. He has the knowledge of everything that's going on and the power to do something about it. It takes effort and time to learn to trust God. You trust him when he's been tested. You trust him when you stop relying on yourself and others as your main strength and support for life.

words
to live by

Things you might not know about *trust:*

● A trust is a separate legal entity that holds assets for the benefit of a person or group, known as the beneficiary. When a trust is established, an individual or corporation called the trustee is entrusted as an overseer. A trustee must be completely relied upon to manage the assets.

● A Gallop poll revealed that nurses are the most trusted professional health care providers in the United States. For being trusted to tell the truth and encouraging confidentiality with the patients, nurses consistently rate above medical doctors.

What is God's message to me in uncertainty? Simply that I must not cast away my confidence. His still voice says, "Trust Me. Put aside your striving, your manipulating, and simply trust Me."
NANCIE CARMICHAEL

Trust the LORD, and do good things. Live in the land, and practice being faithful.
Psalm 37:3
GOD'S WORD

I know God will not give me anything I can't handle. I just wish that He didn't trust me so much.
MOTHER TERESA

God, today I'll trust you. Help me to know and believe some true thing about you. Be my protection in the storms ahead. Be my peace.
Amen.

trust

truth, noun.

1. reality.
2. a fact as the object of correct belief.
3. candor, frankness, honesty.
4. **Biblical:** who God is and all he says.
5. **Personal:** the facts, principles, and promises given by God and revealed in his Word.

t r u t h

Conforming to Facts

Show me your ways, O LORD, teach me your paths; guide me in your truth and teach me, for you are God my Savior, and my hope is in you all day long.
Psalm 25:4–5 NIV

One of the hardest things in life is to be objective about yourself. Most people make excuses about weaknesses or blame others for their problems. If you grew up with parents or other authority figures who allowed you to make excuses, you may be unwilling to take responsibility for your actions. You've been trained to find fault with others instead. You've never learned to face the truth.

Truth is a fixed position, a firm fact established by a recognized authority or proven axiom. Truth forms the stability, the sure foundation, for your life. The Hebrew word *Emunah* means "truthfulness" in contrast to false swearing and lying. The Greek word *alethinos* is true as used of God the Father and God the Son and God's words. God fulfills the meaning of his name as "very God," that is, true to his utterances: he cannot lie. God's Word is truth.

words
to live by

Seekers of truth are hard to find. And truth in a world of uncertainty, chaos, and deception is very difficult to discern without an objective source. The most subjective and prejudiced search for truth is determined through your senses, experiences, and emotions. Even your brain power has its limits. God's Word talks about those intellectuals who are "always learning but never able to acknowledge the truth." In the popular media, propaganda, hype, and spin often win out over truth.

Ask God to guide you in his truth, to teach you. Expose yourself to more of God's Word. Dig deep into it, then allow that truth to penetrate the depths of your heart. God's truth leads, guides, corrects, and reproves you. Believing God's truth will show up in the way you live. Physical evidence of the Lord's deeds can help convince you of the truth of God's Word.

Knowledge of God's truth helps lead you to godly, right living, and walking in God's truth means courage for integrity and honesty in your inmost parts. God's Word provides truth—answers to the meaning of life and who God is. You discover truth about yourself as the Holy Spirit applies God's Word to your heart. No matter how much you claim to be a Christian in public, if privately you practice a secret sin, you're walking in darkness and living a lie. On the other hand, if you claim you have absolutely no sin at all, you're still not living in God's truth.

> To deny reality—or truth—in the name of shielding ourselves or loved ones from criticism or responsibility hurts only those we are trying to help.
> TIM WILDMON

Conforming to Facts

Since you have purified your souls in obeying the truth through the Spirit in sincere love of the brethren, love one another fervently with a pure heart.
I Peter 1:22 NKJV

Not only do you need to know God's truth, but you need to know how to apply it. Truth is more than cold, hard facts. Life pulses behind it. Truth is best spoken with the language of love. You may know that, scientifically, tears contain phosphate of lime, chloride of soda, some mucus, and some water. Facing that truth alone may cause you to discount tears as merely a chemical formula. But there's more to it. Tears are also the expression of either an overjoyed spirit or wounded soul. Truth, when it's combined with love and mercy, offers understanding and personal protection for living in this world of woe.

There's little way to know truth apart from God's Word. It stands as an objective source with God himself as the standard. God's truth must sink into your mind, your soul, and spirit for it to affect your life choices. There's a right way and a wrong way to handle God's truth, always remembering to show mercy and love. If you are violating God's truth, you need to be called to account.

words
to live by

etcetera . . .

Things you might not know about *truth*:

❶ Truth serum is one of a dozen drugs, including barbiturates like sodium amytal, pentothal, and brevital. At one time, these were used as anesthesia for surgery. Doctors started calling them truth serums in the early 1900s when they noticed patients blurting out excessively candid remarks during their use.

❶ Truth is the first victim in a totalitarian government. Truth challenges the legitimacy of power. Press censorship, control of the news media, is often the first sign of trouble.

Adopt a simple rule of behavior: if it's the truth, I'm in; if it's not the truth, count me out.
NEIL ANDERSON

The truth is the kindest thing we can give folks in the end.
HARRIET BEECHER STOWE

We reject all shameful and underhanded methods. We do not try to trick anyone, and we do not distort the word of God. We tell the truth before God.
2 Corinthians 4:2 NLT

truth

God, I want to walk in your truth. Teach me through your Word as I read it today. Show me what truth you want me to deal with.
Amen.

A Supreme Triumph

vic·to·ry, noun.

1. the overcoming of an enemy or any difficulty.
2. the winning of a war.
3. the conquering of evil.
4. *Biblical:* God's final judgment against Satan, sin, and death.
5. *Personal:* dependence upon God's power to pass spiritual tests and overcome trials and temptations.

vic·to·ry

What is the greatest victory in your life? Maybe you lost ten pounds in time for the class reunion. Or maybe you beat out a dozen others for the promotion at work. Perhaps you got to tour Europe before any of your sisters. Or won the marathon race at Seaside. Or just finished the marathon at Seaside. Or you may not think in terms of victory at all. You're more into surviving.

In the Old Testament, *victory* is almost exclusively over external foes that threaten physical peace and security. One of the greatest military victories in the book of Judges happens under the leadership of the prophetess Deborah. None of the men had the courage to lead the Hebrew people against the Canaanites, but she did. Judges 5 is a song of celebration over that great victory.

But in the New Testament, victory expresses mastery over evil. Victory is a very personal triumph as a believer wres-

It was not by their sword that they won the land, nor did their arm bring them victory; it was your right hand, your arm, and the light of your face, for you loved them.
Psalm 44:3 NIV

words
to live by

tles with individual harmful enticements and spiritual assaults. "This is the victory that has overcome the world—our faith" (1 John 5:4). The promise is that those who trust in the power of Jesus will find victory over trials and temptations.

A woman with a sordid reputation burst into the room where Jesus was dining with religious leaders. "Going in, she knelt behind him at his feet, weeping, with her tears falling down upon his feet; and she wiped them off with her hair and kissed them and poured perfume on them" (Luke 7:38). Others complained about her ostentatious behavior, but Jesus knew this was her "victory celebration." Through faith in him, she triumphed over lust and immorality.

Usually, victory equals winning. The stats books record the details, but folks want to know the bottom line, the winners and losers. Who won the election? Who won the basketball game? Who was the finalist in the reality TV series? But that is not true for those committed to following Jesus Christ. Your goal is to be like Jesus, "attaining the whole measure of the fullness of Christ" (Ephesians 4:13). In your journey to that goal there will be obstacles and barriers, trials and tests. Every time any one of these is overcome and you inch (or leap) closer to your

> Far better it is to dare mighty things, to win glorious triumphs even though checkered by failure, than to rank with those poor spirits who neither enjoy nor suffer much because they live in the gray twilight that knows neither victory nor defeat.
> THEODORE ROOSEVELT

grace mercy love faith goodness truth freedom hope
rgiveness peace humble holiness obey repent perfect submit
erve fellowship comforter transformed noble character church

A Supreme Triumph

We will shout for
joy when you are
victorious and will
lift up our banners
in the name of our
God. May the LORD
grant all your
requests.
Psalm 20:5 NIV

goal, it is a victory. And God gives the victory through Jesus. Your most important victories will never be seen by anyone but you and God.

As in any war, every combat-type battle victory requires the right weapons and the knowledge of how to use them. Your spiritual arsenal of weaponry is listed in Ephesians 6:10–18: God's truth, righteousness (integrity and moral fortitude), the gospel of peace (the good news of Jesus), faith, salvation, God's Word, and long, hard praying. No matter how bad things might be right now, no matter how hopeless, you will have victory. You will win by the power of faith, and any and every spiritual victory is worth celebrating.

🔒

Any righteous act done by a child of God constitutes a spiritual victory, from heaven's point of view. You can secure victory in whatever you need to overcome through the power of Christ. With a clear focus on the goal of becoming like Jesus, you can more easily spot your real battles. And armed with the spiritual weapons your faith provides, you will achieve personal victories, large and small.

words
to live by

Things you might not know about *victory*:

1 Upon defeating the Romans at Asculum in 279 B.C., King Pyrrhus remarked, "One more such victory and we are lost." He won the day but lost so many troops that the cause was hopeless. A Pyrrhic victory is one where the losses are so ruinous it is no victory at all.

1 Between 1954 and 1974 many U.S. cities were ringed by Nike missile sites. The ground-to-air missiles were intended to protect against attack by enemy bombers. In Greek, *nike* stands for victory.

Obstacles are those frightful things you see when you take your eyes off your goal.
HENRY FORD

Do you lack victory over sin? This is not to be wondered at if you neglect the Holy Spirit.
F. B. MEYER

Whatever is born of God overcomes the world. And this is the victory that has overcome the world—our faith.
1 John 5:4 NKJV

God, I praise you for your power to give victory to me. Help me know what I need to do today to cooperate with you, to accomplish your spiritual purpose.
Amen.

v · i · c · t · o · r · y

...ss grace mercy love faith goodness truth freedom hope
...rgiveness peace humble holiness obey repent perfect submit
...erve fellowship comforter transformed noble character church

The Anxiety Factor

wor·ry, verb.

1. to feel uneasy, troubled.
2. to be overcome with a nagging concern.
3. to be plagued with doubts.
4. **Biblical:** to have a sinful, willful distraction that pulls your trust away from God.
5. **Personal:** to have an anxiety that you need to unload to God.

w o r · r y

When I said, "My foot is slipping," your love, O LORD, supported me. When anxiety was great within me, your consolation brought joy to my soul.
Psalm 94:18–19 NIV

Eighty-four women sat at lace-covered round tables and finished their crème brûlée while Michelle stared at the back of her spoon. She felt tense. Perspiration beaded her forehead. Finally Sandy leaned over and whispered, "Are you worried about giving the speech?"

"No," Michelle replied. "I'm worried about falling flat on my face before I start it."

Worries swarm like Egyptian plagues all around you. You worry about violence and immorality increasing. You worry about losing too much hair. You worry if important people ignore you. You worry if significant people pay you much attention. You even worry that you worry too much.

In the New Testament, the phrase *do not worry* means "take no thought." For instance, you're to take no thought about what you'll eat or drink or wear or what will happen tomorrow. Instead, think

words
to live by

about seeking God's kingdom and his path of righteousness. That doesn't mean you don't work or plan. But your main emphasis is on other people (God's kingdom) and your spiritual walk (righteousness). That provides plenty to think about and do.

Martha was a faithful, loving, caring follower of Jesus, but she got caught up in a load of worry about the urgent matter of dinner served on time. Her sister, Mary, had it right. She did the one necessary thing—she sat at Jesus' feet. Martha wasn't wrong to tend to the details of dinner, but it didn't have to be done in such a hurry. She could have relaxed with her hospitality, even had one ear cocked toward Jesus, and refrained from scolding Mary.

There's an okay kind of worry that can be helpful, that can lead to positive action. It sets off alarm systems that arouse you to bring aid or get you to an appointment on time. Positive worry overtakes you when something you value is threatened or when you're in the midst of increasing conflict with no resolution in sight and you determine to do something about it.

Toxic worry paralyzes you, makes you useless. Most women worry about things they can do nothing about. Toxic worry consumes the mind so you can't focus on your God-given assignment for the day. Toxic worry captivates like an addiction. It chokes out God's Word. It wears you down, ages you. Toxic worry strangles any good thing that could be growing inside you, like

To worry is to believe that a situation is not under good management. For Christians, the underlying belief is that God cannot handle our needs.
SANDY RUE

Moss grace mercy love faith goodness truth freedom hope
orgiveness peace humble holiness obey repent perfect submit
serve fellowship comforter transformed noble character church

The Anxiety Factor

faith or courage or compassion.

An antidote for toxic worry comes from Philippians: Rejoice, delight yourself in the Lord. Allow God's peace to flood over you and guard your heart and mind from all that worry.

You have a choice: to develop your trust in God or to increase your worry. Determine to convert your worry to faith by productive action. Meditate on God, upon all the reasons you can place your full confidence in him. Faith tells worry that God is good, all the time. Faith tells worry that God will give you hope. Faith tells worry that God is active right now on your behalf.

> Humble yourselves under the mighty hand of God, that He may exalt you in due time.
> I Peter 5:6 NKJV

❶

Worry strangles trust and throttles faith. You do your spiritual part of developing faith and trust, and God provides your necessities. God cares about your worry, so give it to him. Worry is a distracting care. To be free of worry is to be free of a major distraction to your emotional, mental, and spiritual life. Refuse to fret. Get in close communion with God.

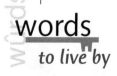

words
to live by

etcetera . . .

Things you might not know about *worry:*

❶ Probably the most widely used measure of worry is the Penn State Worry Questionnaire, which was designed to capture the generality, excessiveness, and uncontrollability characteristic of pathological worry. Individuals with generalized anxiety disorder (GAD) score higher on the questionnaire than those with other anxiety disorders.

❶ Medical research has proven that worry breaks down the immune system and renders the body incapable of resisting disease. Worry causes sleepless nights that weaken your body's effectiveness. Worry damages the nervous system, especially the digestive organs and the heart.

Worry is concern about something that one can do nothing about, and that one cannot even be sure about. That is why it tears us apart.
JAY E. ADAMS

Of all the joy stealers that can plague our lives, none is more nagging, more agitating, or more prevalent than worry.
CHARLES SWINDOLL

God will help you deal with whatever hard things come up when the time comes.
Matthew 6:34
THE MESSAGE

God, I want your peace and joy. Help me release my worries, one by one, to you right now. Take the burden of them from me and clear my mind to take positive steps to take care of them.
Amen.

w o r r y

Blessed the woman, who listens to me,
awake and ready for me each morning,
alert and responsive.

🔒

Proverbs 8:34 THE MESSAGE